SharePoint 2013

Enterprise Search

Walkthrough Guide

Hands-On Lab Edition

STEVEN MANN

SharePoint 2013 Enterprise Search Walkthrough Guide - Hands-On Lab Edition

Copyright © 2013 by Steven Mann

Trademarks

Screenshots of Microsoft Products and Services

Warning and Disclaimer

Cover By: David H. Ross (http://davidhross.com/)

Introduction

Enterprise Search in SharePoint 2013 Server provides an abundance of functionality and search capabilities for your SharePoint environment. It can be very overwhelming when trying to setup, configure, and understand all of the many search features and processes.

Therefore, I have provided an easy step-by-step hands-on lab guide to walk you through the necessary steps to help facilitate the creation and functionality of your Search Center site.

With this walkthrough guide approach, you can see what options and selections are necessary without having to read all of the steps. Many find it easier to see what someone is trying to do rather than picture in their head or stumble through a screen to find the appropriate selections.

I hope you find this lab guide useful and if you have any questions or other twists that I do not address, please send me an email (steve@stevethemanmann.com) and I will be glad to assist you.

Stay updated with my blog posts: www.SteveTheManMann.com

Reference links and source code is available on www.stevethemanmann.com:

Creating the Search Service Application and Crawling Content

This Lab walks you through the steps for creating your Search Service Application. This may be performed via Central Admin or via PowerShell. Both approaches are outlined however I recommend using PowerShell scripting as it provides more options and control. Once your Search Topology is initially created, you need to use PowerShell anyway if you wish to scale out your components.

Enterprise Search has various Search Components which may be scaled out on your farm. These Search Components require a large amount of resources so it is important to understand the grand scheme. I would review the Enterprise Search architectures available here:

http://go.microsoft.com/fwlink/p/?LinkId=259182

Link available on www.stevethemanmann.com on the Reference Links and Source Code page.

Task 1-1A: Create the Search Service Application via Central Administration

1	Launch Central Administration and select Manage service applications link under Application Management.	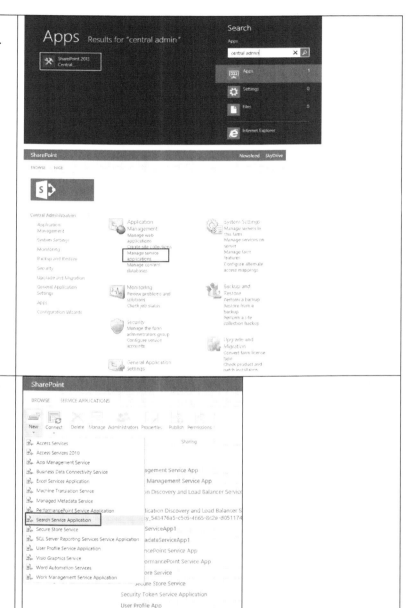
2	From the New menu, select Search Service Application	

3	Review the dialog that appears	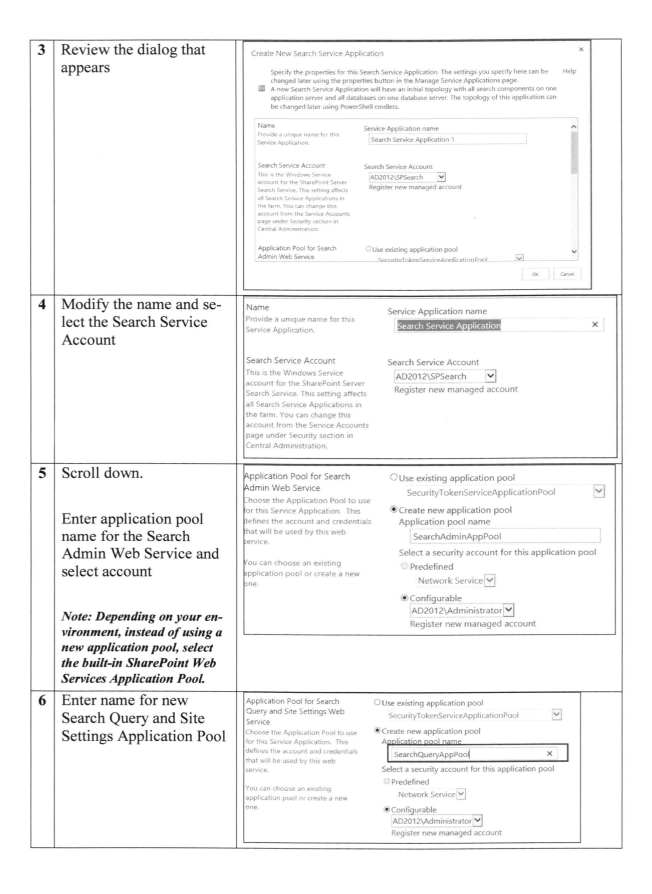

Create New Search Service Application   ×

Specify the properties for this Search Service Application. The settings you specify here can be   Help
changed later using the properties button in the Manage Service Applications page.

A new Search Service Application will have an initial topology with all search components on one
application server and all databases on one database server. The topology of this application can
be changed later using PowerShell cmdlets.

Name   Service Application name
Provide a unique name for this
Service Application.   [Search Service Application 1]

Search Service Account   Search Service Account
This is the Windows Service
account for the SharePoint Server   [AD2012\SPSearch ▾]
Search Service. This setting affects   Register new managed account
all Search Service Applications in
the farm. You can change this
account from the Service Accounts
page under Security section in
Central Administration.

Application Pool for Search   ○ Use existing application pool
Admin Web Service   SecurityTokenServiceApplicationPool

                                                    OK   Cancel

4	Modify the name and select the Search Service Account	Name Provide a unique name for this Service Application. Service Application name [Search Service Application] × Search Service Account This is the Windows Service account for the SharePoint Server Search Service. This setting affects all Search Service Applications in the farm. You can change this account from the Service Accounts page under Security section in Central Administration. Search Service Account [AD2012\SPSearch ▾] Register new managed account

5	Scroll down. Enter application pool name for the Search Admin Web Service and select account *Note: Depending on your environment, instead of using a new application pool, select the built-in SharePoint Web Services Application Pool.*	Application Pool for Search Admin Web Service Choose the Application Pool to use for this Service Application. This defines the account and credentials that will be used by this web service. You can choose an existing application pool or create a new one. ○ Use existing application pool SecurityTokenServiceApplicationPool ▾ ● Create new application pool Application pool name [SearchAdminAppPool] Select a security account for this application pool ○ Predefined Network Service ▾ ● Configurable AD2012\Administrator ▾ Register new managed account

6	Enter name for new Search Query and Site Settings Application Pool	Application Pool for Search Query and Site Settings Web Service Choose the Application Pool to use for this Service Application. This defines the account and credentials that will be used by this web service. You can choose an existing application pool or create a new one. ○ Use existing application pool SecurityTokenServiceApplicationPool ▾ ● Create new application pool Application pool name [SearchQueryAppPool] × Select a security account for this application pool ○ Predefined Network Service ▾ ● Configurable AD2012\Administrator ▾ Register new managed account

| 7 | Click OK. |  |

The Search Service Application begins creation:

Create New Search Service Application

Please wait while your changes are processed for Search Service Application.

Task 1-1B: Create the Search Service Application via PowerShell

It is recommended to use PowerShell to create your Search Service Application as it provides more flexibility and control over what and where things are created. Praveen Hebbar provided a great guideline here:

http://blogs.technet.com/b/praveenh/archive/2013/02/07/create-a-new-search-service-application-in-sharepoint-2013-using-powershell.aspx

(You can get the reference link at stevethemanmann.com)

1	Create a PowerShell Script using the reference
2	Launch PowerShell or the SharePoint 2013 Management Console
3	Run the script to create the Search Service Application

You may run this in PowerShell itself since the first line loads the SharePoint add-in, or you may run it using the SharePoint 2013 Management Console.

Task 1-2: View the Results of the Search Service Application Creation

After the Search Service Application is created, you may you use Get-SPServiceApplication in the SharePoint 2013 Management Shell to see that it was created or simply view the Service Applications in Central Admin:

1	Use Get-SPServiceApplication in the SharePoint 2013 Management Shell	
2	View the Service Applications in Central Admin	
3	Use Get-SPDatabase from the SharePoint 2013 Management Shell to review the databases created for Search	

| 4 | Open SQL Server Management Studio and connect to the SharePoint SQL Server. Expand the databases folder to review the databases created. |  |

Task 1-3: Crawl Local SharePoint Content

You can't search for anything without first crawling the content. Here are the steps:

1	Navigate to Central Administration and click on Manage service applications	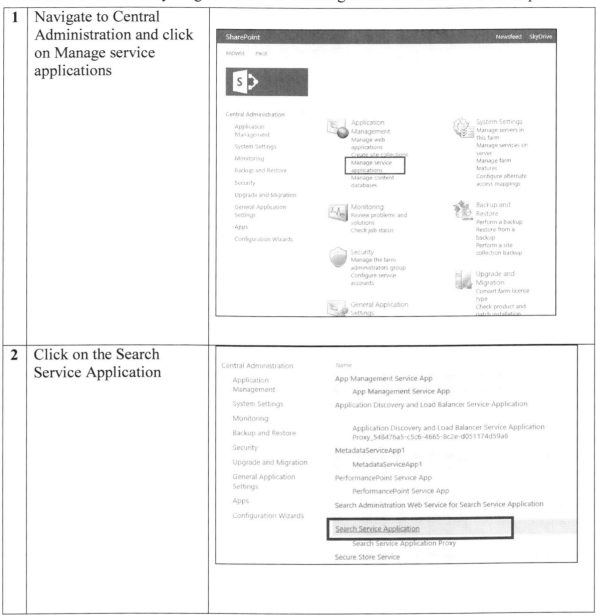
2	Click on the Search Service Application	

3	Click on Content Sources	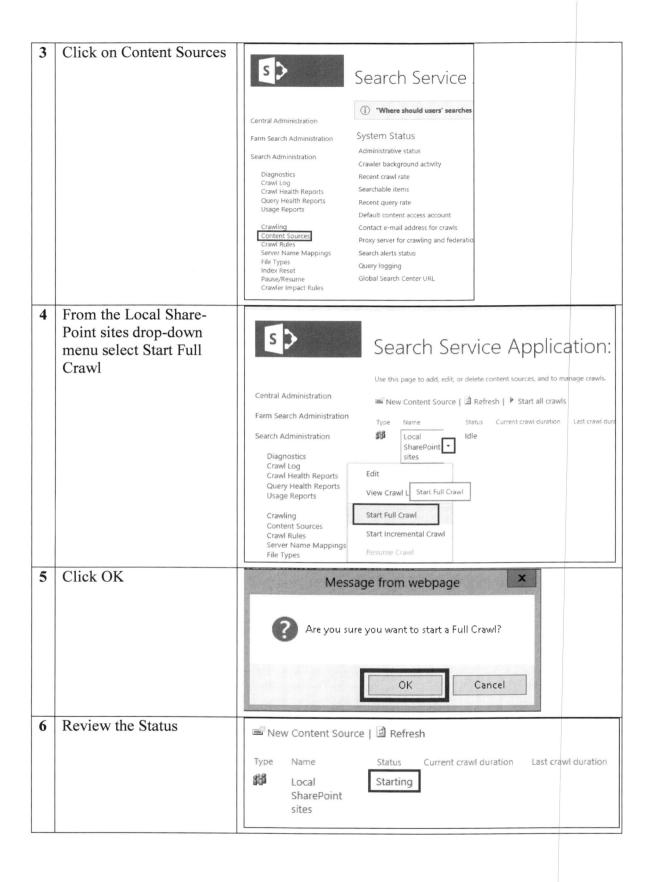
4	From the Local Share-Point sites drop-down menu select Start Full Crawl	
5	Click OK	
6	Review the Status	

7	Click Refresh to update the content source status	Use this page to add, edit, or delete content sources, and to manage crawls. New Content Source | Refresh | Stop all crawls | Pause all crawls Type Name Status Current crawl duration Last crawl duration Last crawl completed Local SharePoint sites — Crawling Full — 00:01:03
8	Once the Status is Idle again, the crawl is complete	Type Name Status Current crawl duration Last crawl duration Last crawl completed Local SharePoint sites — Idle — — 00:07:49 — 3/30/2013 4:17:30 PM Crawl Complete

Creating and Configuring a Search Center

This lab walks you through the steps for creating your Search Center. The Search Center is a site collection that may be used as a central location for users to perform searches. Once the Search Center is created, the Service Application and other sites need to know where it lives such that search queries may be directed to it.

Task 2-1: Create an Enterprise Search Center Site Collection

It is recommended to create a central Search Center site collection that presents the search results to users. It is easier to maintain and control one central location for search presentation. Therefore follow the steps in this task section to create your Search Center site collection.

1	Launch Central Admin	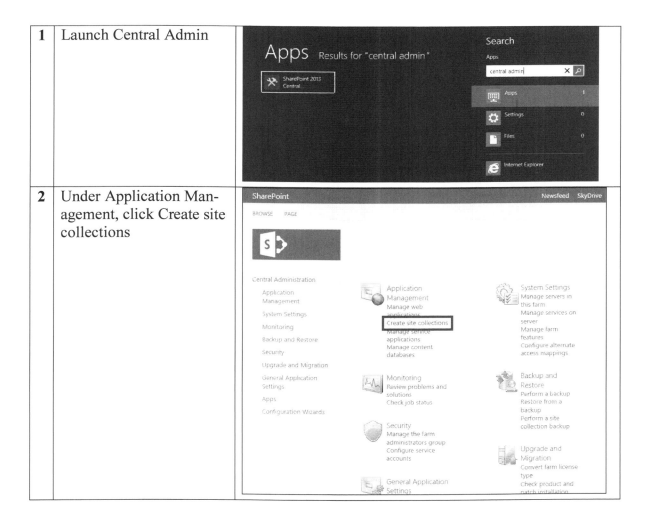
2	Under Application Management, click Create site collections	

3	Enter a title and URL for your Search Center	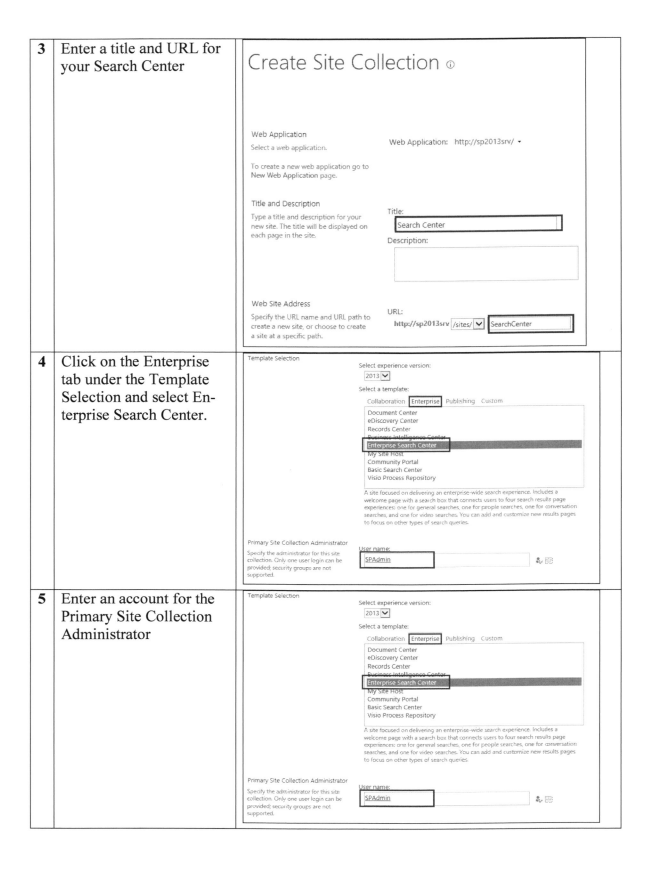 **Create Site Collection** ⓘ **Web Application** Select a web application. To create a new web application go to New Web Application page. Web Application: http://sp2013srv/ ▾ **Title and Description** Type a title and description for your new site. The title will be displayed on each page in the site. Title: Search Center Description: **Web Site Address** Specify the URL name and URL path to create a new site, or choose to create a site at a specific path. URL: http://sp2013srv /sites/ ▾ SearchCenter
4	Click on the Enterprise tab under the Template Selection and select Enterprise Search Center.	Template Selection Select experience version: 2013 ▾ Select a template: Collaboration Enterprise Publishing Custom Document Center eDiscovery Center Records Center Business Intelligence Center Enterprise Search Center My Site Host Community Portal Basic Search Center Visio Process Repository A site focused on delivering an enterprise-wide search experience. Includes a welcome page with a search box that connects users to four search results page experiences: one for general searches, one for people searches, one for conversation searches, and one for video searches. You can add and customize new results pages to focus on other types of search queries. Primary Site Collection Administrator Specify the administrator for this site collection. Only one user login can be provided; security groups are not supported. User name: SPAdmin
5	Enter an account for the Primary Site Collection Administrator	Template Selection Select experience version: 2013 ▾ Select a template: Collaboration Enterprise Publishing Custom Document Center eDiscovery Center Records Center Business Intelligence Center Enterprise Search Center My Site Host Community Portal Basic Search Center Visio Process Repository A site focused on delivering an enterprise-wide search experience. Includes a welcome page with a search box that connects users to four search results page experiences: one for general searches, one for people searches, one for conversation searches, and one for video searches. You can add and customize new results pages to focus on other types of search queries. Primary Site Collection Administrator Specify the administrator for this site collection. Only one user login can be provided; security groups are not supported. User name: SPAdmin

6	Click OK. Your new Search Center site collection begins creation. It shouldn't take *too* long. After a minute or two your site collection is ready.	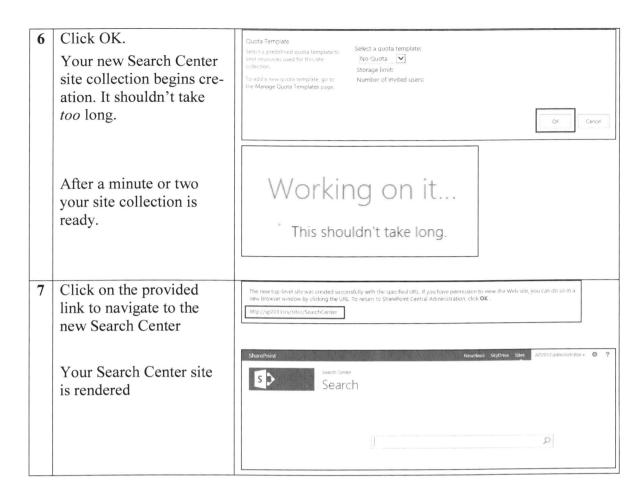
7	Click on the provided link to navigate to the new Search Center Your Search Center site is rendered	The new top-level site was created successfully with the specified URL. If you have permission to view the Web site, you can do so in a new browser window by clicking the URL. To return to SharePoint Central Administration, click **OK**. http://sp2013srv/sites/SearchCenter

Task 2-2: Test Your Search Center

1	Navigate to your Search Center. Enter a search term and click the search button	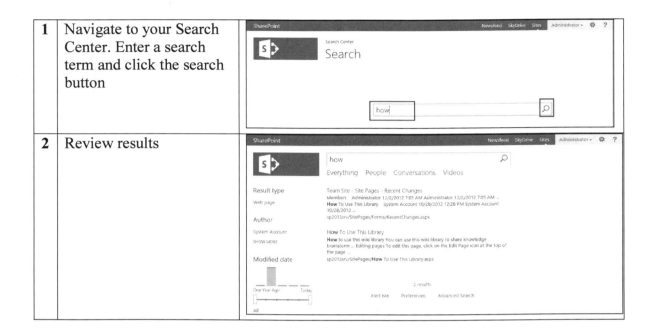
2	Review results	

Task 2-3 Configure Sites to Use Your Search Center

NOTE If you set the global Search Center setting in your Search Service Application, as explained in the next task section, you do not need to configure each site separately.

1	Navigate to your main (root) site collection	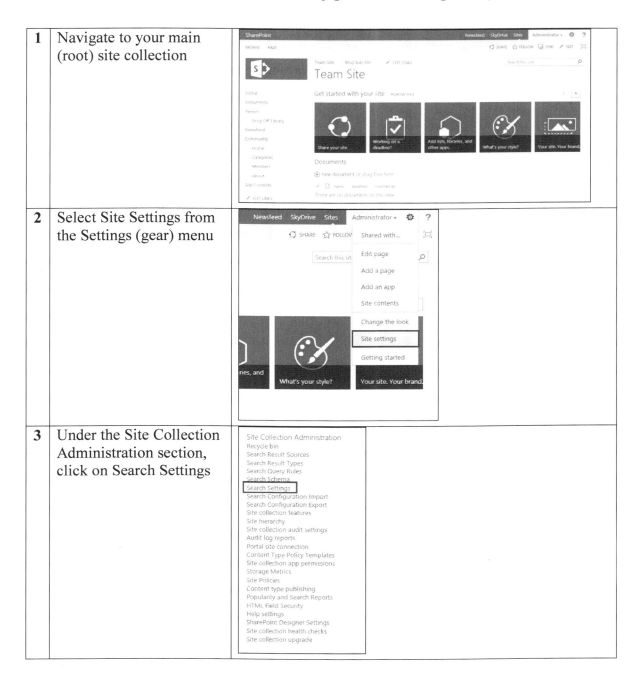
2	Select Site Settings from the Settings (gear) menu	
3	Under the Site Collection Administration section, click on Search Settings	

4	Enter your Search Center URL. Make sure you include /Pages at the end	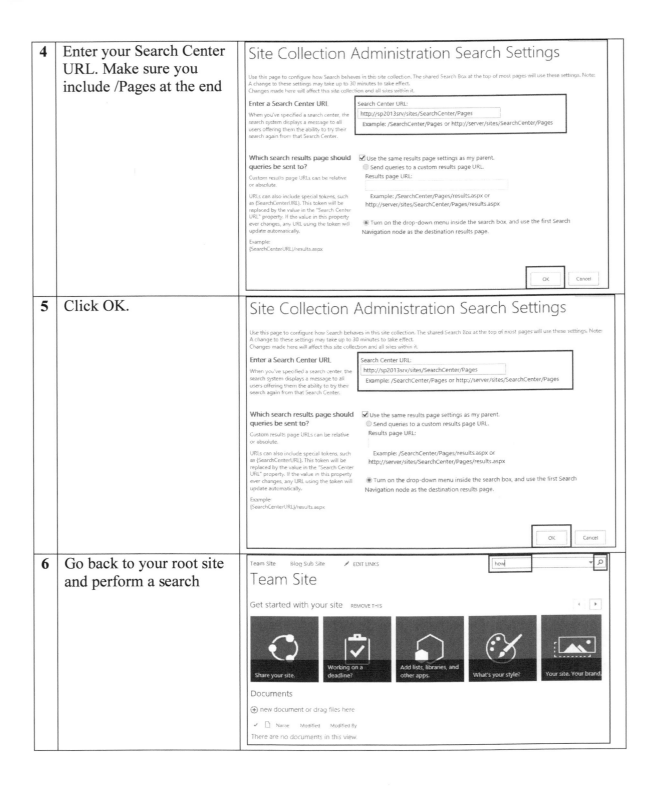
5	Click OK.	
6	Go back to your root site and perform a search	

| 7 | The local results are displayed

Examine the "expand your search" link. It now points to your Search Center | 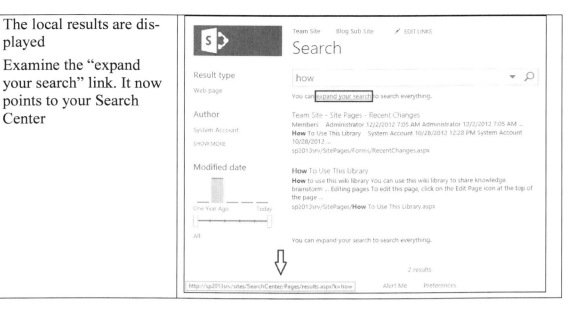 |

Team Site   Blog Sub Site   ✏ EDIT LINKS

Search

Result type
Web page

how   ▼ 🔍

You can expand your search to search everything.

Author
System Account
SHOW MORE

Team Site - Site Pages - Recent Changes
Members   Administrator 12/2/2012 7:05 AM Administrator 12/2/2012 7:05 AM ...
How To Use This Library   System Account 10/28/2012 12:28 PM System Account 10/28/2012 ...
sp2013srv/SitePages/Forms/RecentChanges.aspx

Modified date

How To Use This Library
How to use this wiki library You can use this wiki library to share knowledge, brainstorm ... Editing pages To edit this page, click on the Edit Page icon at the top of the page ...
sp2013srv/SitePages/**How** To Use This Library.aspx

One Year Ago   Today

All

You can expand your search to search everything.

2 results

http://sp2013srv/sites/SearchCenter/Pages/results.aspx?k=how   Alert Me   Preferences

Task 2-4: Configure the Search Service Application to Use Your Search Center

1	Navigate to Central Administration and click on Manage service applications	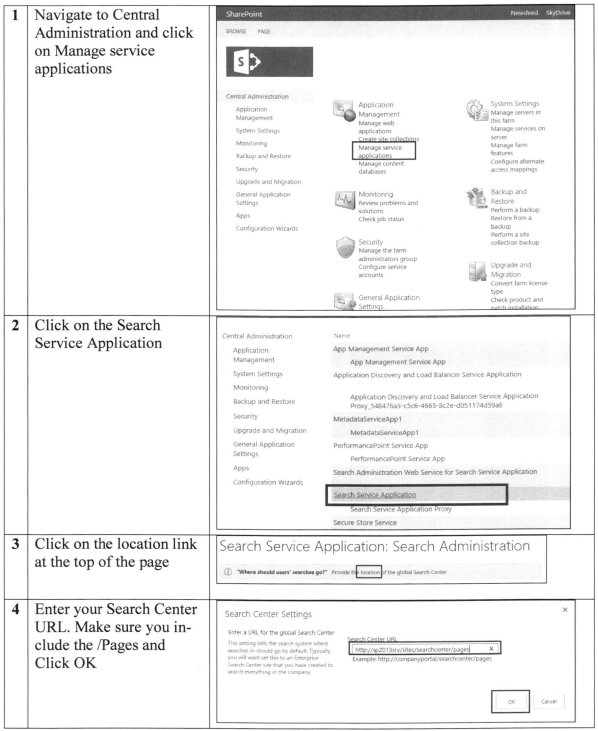
2	Click on the Search Service Application	
3	Click on the location link at the top of the page	
4	Enter your Search Center URL. Make sure you include the /Pages and Click OK	

By setting this, all of your site collections will automatically use the global Search Center setting. *Thus, you do not need to configure each site collection separately.*

LAB 3

Configuring the Search Web Parts

This lab walks through the search web parts that appear within the results pages of your Search Center. Additional modification and configuration steps are outlined in later labs.

Task 3-1: Modify the Search Center Default Page

Before the results pages are modified, the main page of the Search Center may be tweaked by modifying the Search Box web part on that page.

1	Navigate to your Search Center	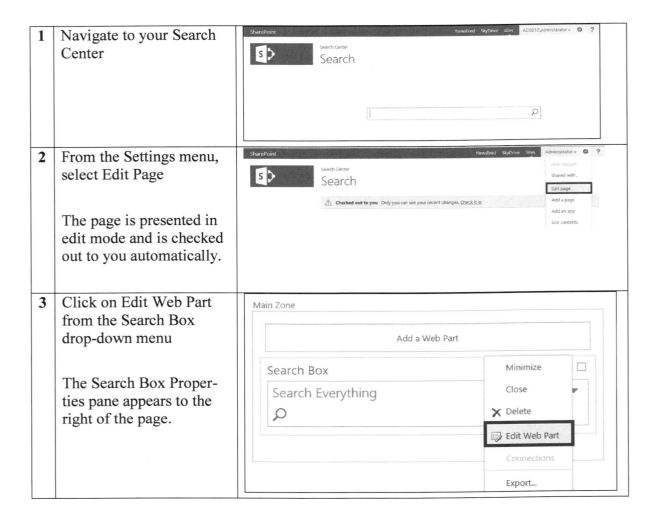
2	From the Settings menu, select Edit Page The page is presented in edit mode and is checked out to you automatically.	
3	Click on Edit Web Part from the Search Box drop-down menu The Search Box Properties pane appears to the right of the page.	

4	Select the Turn on drop-down Search Navigation option	◀ Search Box ✕
		
		Properties for Search Box ⌃
		
		⊟ Which search results page should queries be sent to? Help
		
		☐ Use this site's Search Settings
		○ Send queries to other Web Parts on this page.
		○ Send queries to a custom results page URL.
		    Results page URL:
		    results.aspx
		
		◉ Turn on the drop-down Search Navigation menu inside the search box, and use the first navigation node as the destination results page.

5	Click OK.	Help URL [ ] Help Mode [Modeless ▾] Catalog Icon Image URL [ ] Title Icon Image URL [ ] Import Error Message [Cannot import this Web Part.] Target Audiences [ ] 👥 ▥ [OK] [Cancel] [Apply]
6	Check in the page	
7	Publish the page	

Now the user has an option to search within a defined context and navigate directly to that results page. These were previously named "scopes". Clicking Enter or clicking on the search button (magnifying glass) sends the query to the Everything page (results.aspx) by default if no other selection is made..

Search

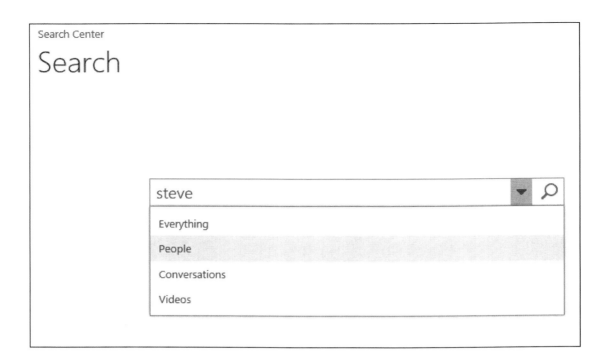

steve

Everything

People

Conversations

Videos

Task 3-2: Review the Search Results Pages

The Search Center site collection is created with predefined search results pages. By default, the visible result pages configured via the navigation are as follows

Everything	results.aspx
People	peopleresults.aspx
Conversations	conversationresults.aspx
Videos	videoresults.aspx

There is also a reports and data results page as well as an advanced search page. You may review the pages by following these steps:

1	Navigate to your Search Center and select Site Contents from the Settings menu	
2	Double-click the Pages app	

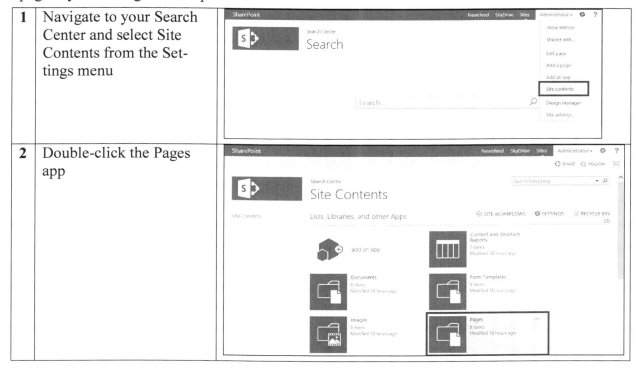

| 3 | Review the various pages available | 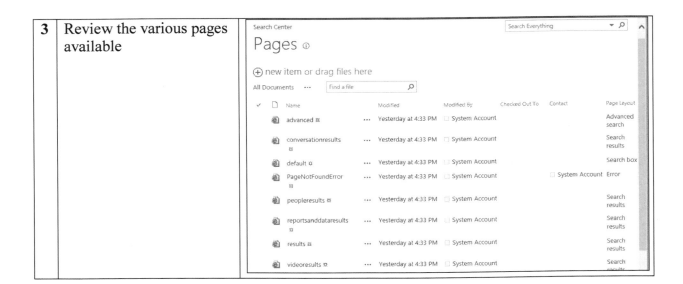 |

Task 3-3: Modify the Search Results Pages

1	Click on one of the results pages in the Pages library or perform a search from your Search Center to get to the main results page	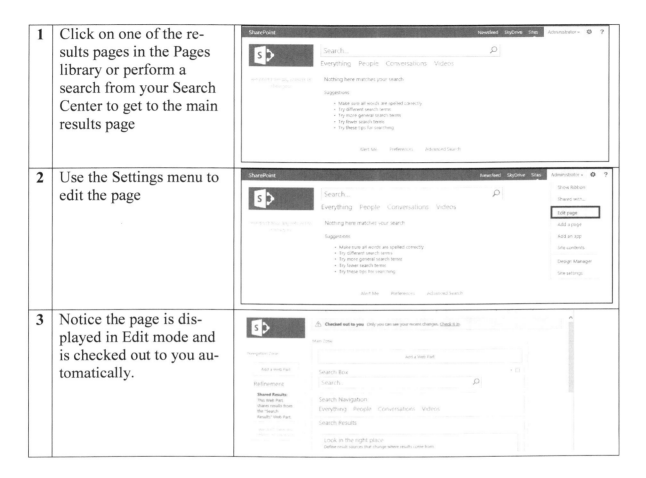
2	Use the Settings menu to edit the page	
3	Notice the page is displayed in Edit mode and is checked out to you automatically.	

The next tasks walk through the modification of the web parts on the results page.

Task 3-4: Modify the Search Box Web Part

1	Once your page is in Edit Mode as explained in the previous task section, use the drop-down menu on the Search Box web part to modify the settings. Click on Edit Web Part from the Search Box drop-down menu	Search Box Search... Search Navigation Everything People Conversations Videos Search Results Look in the right place Minimize Close ✕ Delete ▣ Edit Web Part Connections Export...

2	Review the Search Box Properties pane to the right.
	
	By default, each Search Box on each results page sends the queries to the Search Results web part on the same page. Use this first section of the Search Box properties to modify that behavior if needed. This is usually performed on pages that have a Search Box but is not displaying the results on the same page. An example would be the Search Center default page as explained the previous section. *So there is no need to modify this first group of settings on a results page Search Box web part.*
		◀ Search Box ✕
		Properties for Search Box ⌃
		
		☐ Which search results page Help
		should queries be sent to?
		   ☐ Use this site's Search Settings
		   ◉ Send queries to other
		   Web Parts on this page.
		      ☑ Search Results -
		      Default
		   ○ Send queries to a custom
		   results page URL.
		      Results page URL:
		      /sites/SearchCenter/Pages/
		
		   ○ Turn on the drop-down
		   Search Navigation menu
		   inside the search box, and
		   use the first navigation node	

3	Expand the Query Suggestions section	Query Suggestions Help
		☑ Show suggestions
		☐ Show people name suggestions
	By default the Search Box is set to show suggestions. You may also elect to show people name suggestions. This provides functionality similar to an auto-complete. You may configure how many suggestions appear and how long it takes to show suggestions based on the number of minimum characters configured.	Number of query suggestions
		5
		Minimum number of characters
		2
		Suggestions delay (in milliseconds)
		100
	When a user searches for an item over and over again, the results that they select become part of their personal favorites. You may elect to turn off this functionality by unchecking the Show personal favorites results checkbox, or you may configure how many personal favorites appear.	☑ Show personal favorite results
		Number of personal favorites
		3

4	Expand the Settings section. The Show preferences link option displays a link next to the Search Box where users may modify their search experience. The Show advanced link also displays a link to the right of the Search Box and navigates the user to the advanced search page.	⊟ Settings Help ☑ Show preferences link ☑ Show advanced link Advanced search page URL advanced.aspx Search box control Display Template Default Search Box ▾ Customize Control Display Templates ☑ Make the search box have focus when the page is loaded	
5	Locate the Make the search box have focus when the page is loaded check box. This places the cursor inside the search box so you do not have to click inside to make a change.	⊟ Settings Help ☑ Show preferences link ☑ Show advanced link Advanced search page URL advanced.aspx Search box control Display Template Default Search Box ▾ Customize Control Display Templates ☑ Make the search box have focus when the page is loaded	

6	Make any changes to the Search Box properties to review the behavior and click OK	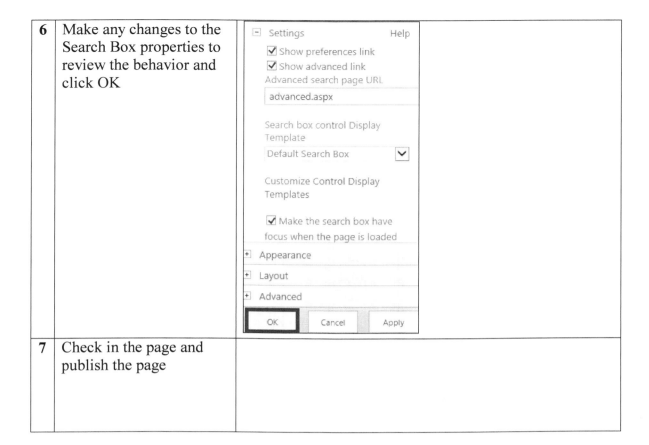	
7	Check in the page and publish the page		

Task 3-5: Modify the Search Navigation Web Part

You do not modify the Search Navigation web part to modify the actual search navigation. You simply modify the web part to alter the display of the search navigation pages. Modification of the search navigation in your Search Center is explained in Lab 4.

1	Navigate to a results page and use the Settings menu to edit the page	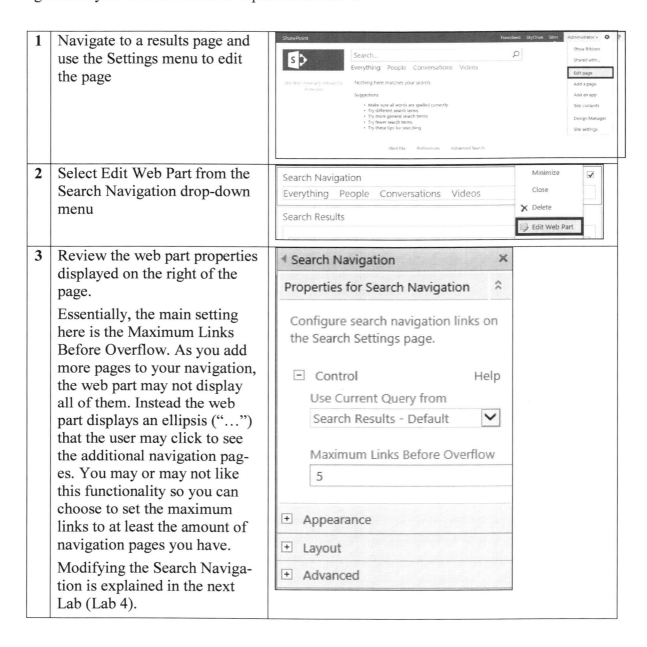
2	Select Edit Web Part from the Search Navigation drop-down menu	
3	Review the web part properties displayed on the right of the page. Essentially, the main setting here is the Maximum Links Before Overflow. As you add more pages to your navigation, the web part may not display all of them. Instead the web part displays an ellipsis ("...") that the user may click to see the additional navigation pages. You may or may not like this functionality so you can choose to set the maximum links to at least the amount of navigation pages you have. Modifying the Search Navigation is explained in the next Lab (Lab 4).	

Task 3-6: Modify the Search Results Web Part

1	Navigate to a results page and use the Settings menu to edit the page	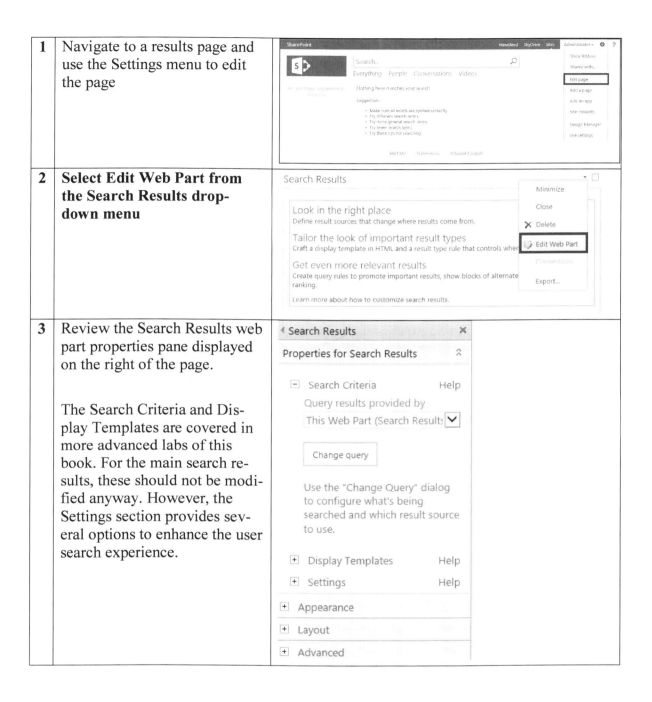
2	**Select Edit Web Part from the Search Results drop-down menu**	
3	Review the Search Results web part properties pane displayed on the right of the page. The Search Criteria and Display Templates are covered in more advanced labs of this book. For the main search results, these should not be modified anyway. However, the Settings section provides several options to enhance the user search experience.	

4	Expand the Settings section The default number of results is 10. You may increase this to a maximum of 50. The next few settings are to show various search options to the user. You do not need to show the link to the search center since you are already in the Search Center. This option is for Search Results that may be on another site. The Show advanced link is similar to the Search Box web part but determines if the Advanced link is shown at the bottom of the results	☐ Settings Help **Results settings** Number of results per page \[10 \] ☑ Show ranked results ☑ Show promoted results ☑ Show "Did you mean?" ☑ Show personal favorites ☐ Show View Duplicates link ☐ Show link to search center Specify the search center in Search Settings **Results control settings** ☑ Show advanced link Advanced search page URL \[advanced.aspx \]
5	Scroll down for more settings The Show result count option determines if the result count is displayed in the search results The Show sort dropdown option allows the user to sort the search results. The customization of the sort dropdown is covered in Lab 11. This option displays a dropdown in the search results for sorting purposes The Show paging option allows users to go to the next page of results. The Show preferences link option determines if the Preferences link is displayed within the Search Results	☑ Show result count ☑ Show language dropdown ☑ Show sort dropdown Available sort orders (JSON) \[{"name":"Relevance","sorts": []},{"name":"Date (Newest)","sorts": [{"p":"Write","d":1}]}, {"name":"Date \] ☑ Show paging ☑ Show preferences link ☑ Show AlertMe link ⊞ Appearance ⊞ Layout ⊞ Advanced [OK] [Cancel] [Apply]

	The Show alertme link option determines if the Alert Me link is displayed within the Search Results	
6	Click OK in the web part properties to save the changes to the Search Results web part	⊞ Display Templates Help ⊞ Settings Help ⊞ Appearance ⊞ Layout ⊞ Advanced **OK** Cancel Apply
7	Check in and publish the page	

YOU WILL NEED TO MAKE SIMILAR CHANGES TO THE OTHER RESULT PAGES FOR CONSISTENCY.

Task 3-7: Modify the Refinement Web Part

1	Navigate to a results page and use the Settings menu to edit the page	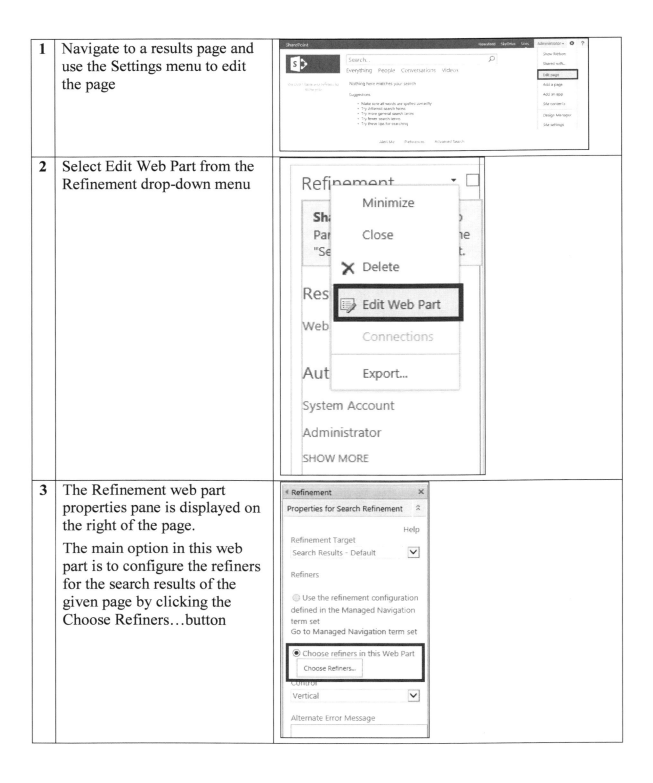
2	Select Edit Web Part from the Refinement drop-down menu	
3	The Refinement web part properties pane is displayed on the right of the page. The main option in this web part is to configure the refiners for the search results of the given page by clicking the Choose Refiners…button	

| 4 | Review the Refinement configuration dialog

The top section allows you to add or remove refinement properties as well as order them accordingly. The bottom section configures how the refinement is displayed and sorted. Customization of the refinements is explained in Lab 11. | 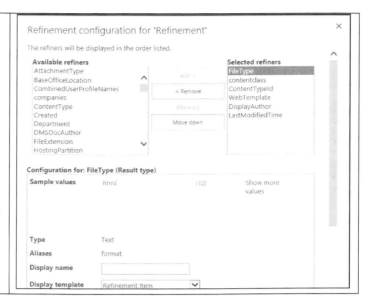 |

Configuring the Search Navigation

This Lab walks through modifying and configuring the Search Navigation.

Task 4-1: Access the Search Navigation Configuration Page

1	Navigate to your Search Center and select Site Settings from the Settings menu	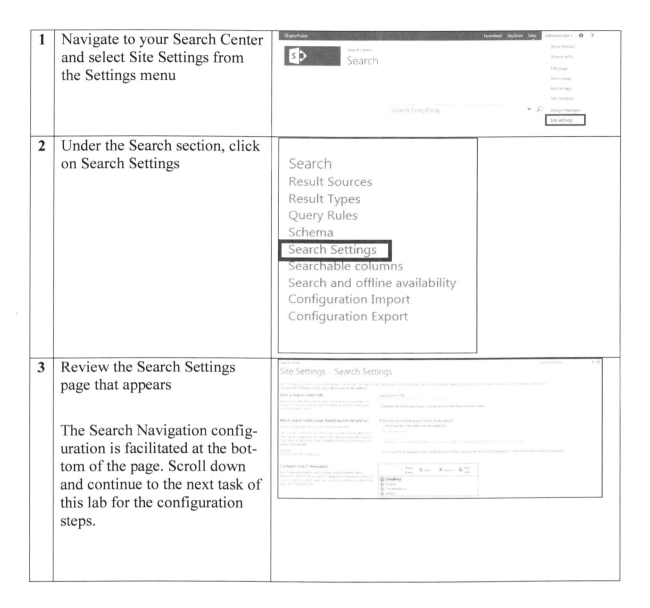
2	Under the Search section, click on Search Settings	
3	Review the Search Settings page that appears The Search Navigation configuration is facilitated at the bottom of the page. Scroll down and continue to the next task of this lab for the configuration steps.	

Task 4-2: Configure the Search Navigation

The Search Navigation configuration is located at the bottom of the Search Settings page for the current Site

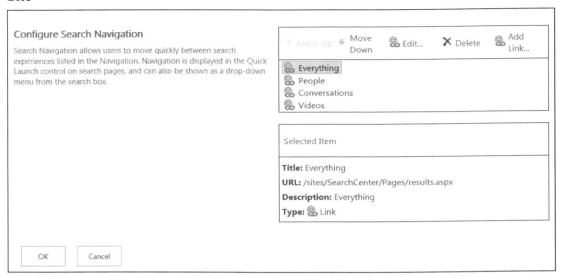

1	Click on Add Link... The Navigation Link dialog appears.	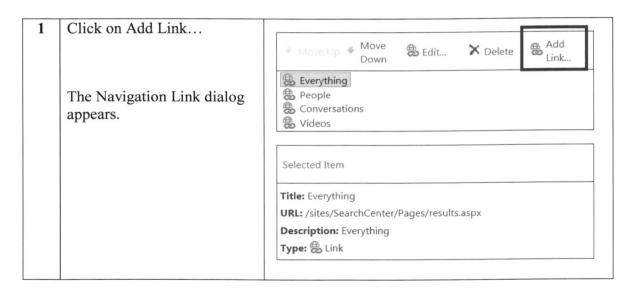

2	Enter Reports as the title and /sites/SearchCenter/Pages/reportsanddataresults.aspx as the URL	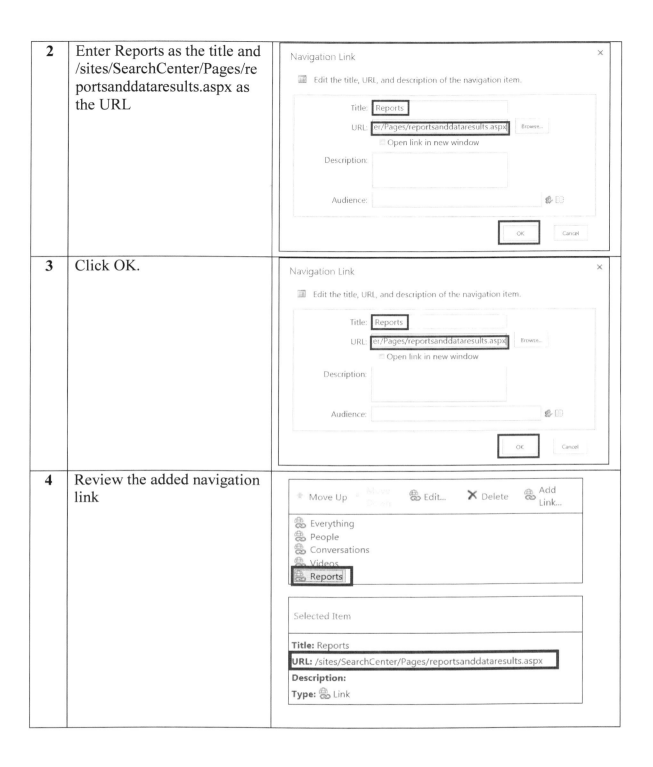
3	Click OK.	
4	Review the added navigation link	

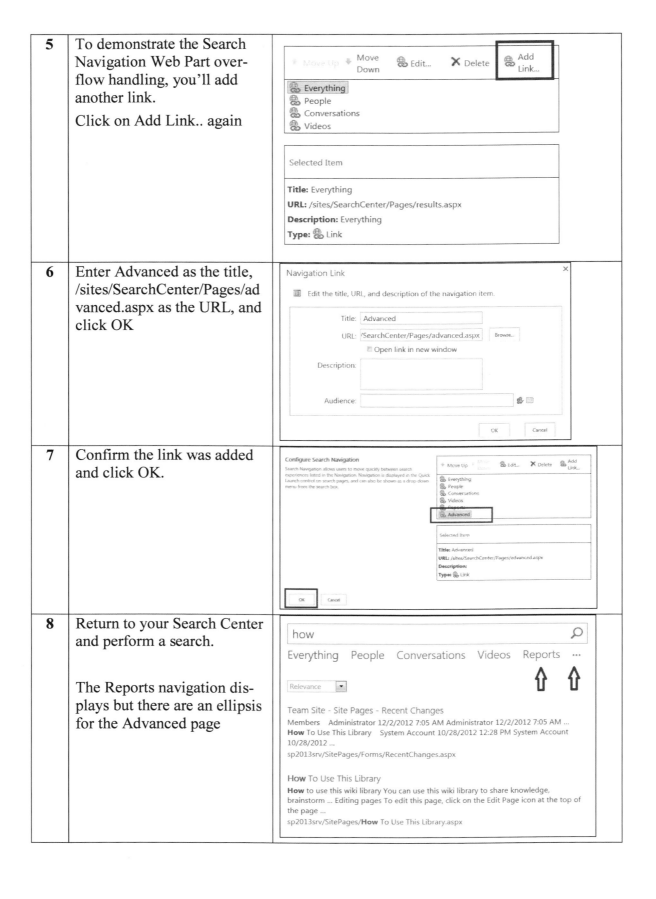

5	To demonstrate the Search Navigation Web Part over-flow handling, you'll add another link. Click on Add Link.. again	
6	Enter Advanced as the title, /sites/SearchCenter/Pages/advanced.aspx as the URL, and click OK	
7	Confirm the link was added and click OK.	
8	Return to your Search Center and perform a search. The Reports navigation displays but there are an ellipsis for the Advanced page	

Step 5 image contents:

Move Up Move Down Edit... Delete Add Link...

Everything
People
Conversations
Videos

Selected Item

Title: Everything
URL: /sites/SearchCenter/Pages/results.aspx
Description: Everything
Type: Link

Step 6 image contents:

Navigation Link

Edit the title, URL, and description of the navigation item.

Title: Advanced
URL: /SearchCenter/Pages/advanced.aspx   Browse...
Open link in new window
Description:
Audience:

OK   Cancel

Step 7 image contents:

Configure Search Navigation

Search Navigation allows users to move quickly between search experiences listed in the Navigation. Navigation is displayed in the Quick Launch control on search pages, and can also be shown as a drop-down menu from the search box.

Move Up Move Down Edit... Delete Add Link...

Everything
People
Conversations
Videos
Reports
Advanced

Selected Item

Title: Advanced
URL: /sites/SearchCenter/Pages/advanced.aspx
Description:
Type: Link

OK   Cancel

Step 8 image contents:

how

Everything People Conversations Videos Reports ...

Relevance

Team Site - Site Pages - Recent Changes
Members   Administrator 12/2/2012 7:05 AM Administrator 12/2/2012 7:05 AM ...
How To Use This Library   System Account 10/28/2012 12:28 PM System Account 10/28/2012 ...
sp2013srv/SitePages/Forms/RecentChanges.aspx

How To Use This Library
How to use this wiki library You can use this wiki library to share knowledge, brainstorm ... Editing pages To edit this page, click on the Edit Page icon at the top of the page ...
sp2013srv/SitePages/How To Use This Library.aspx

9	Click on the ellipsis (…) to show the Advanced page. This is based on the setting in the Search Navigation web part that was explained in Lab 3.	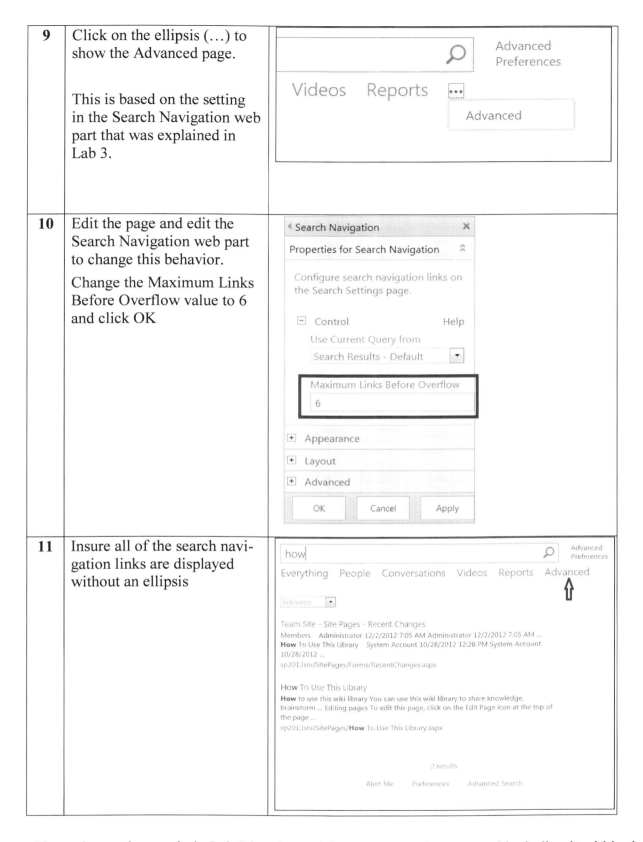
10	Edit the page and edit the Search Navigation web part to change this behavior. Change the Maximum Links Before Overflow value to 6 and click OK	
11	Insure all of the search navigation links are displayed without an ellipsis	

The end-to-end scenario in Lab 9 involves adding a new results page and including it within the navigation. **Although the navigation flows through to all search results pages within the site, the overflow setting does not. Therefore, you need to modify the Search Navigation web part on each search result page within your Search Center site.**

Modifying the Image Display Hover Panel

Hovering over the image search results does not show a larger preview image:

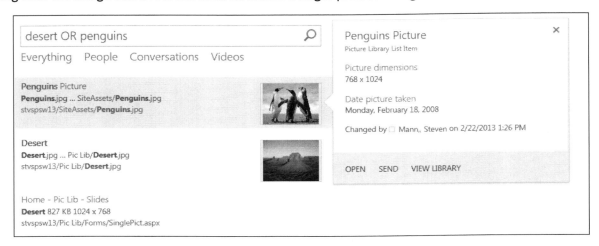

This lab walks through the modification of the image hover panel such that a preview is displayed.

1	Launch SharePoint Designer 2013 and Open the Search Center Site	
2	Click on All Files from the left-hand navigation If you attempt to get the files from the Master Pages, you will not see any items once you get to the Display Templates folders. A list of all files is displayed in the main window.	
3	Double-click on the _catalogs folder in the main window	

4	Review the _catalogs structure under the left-hand navigation.	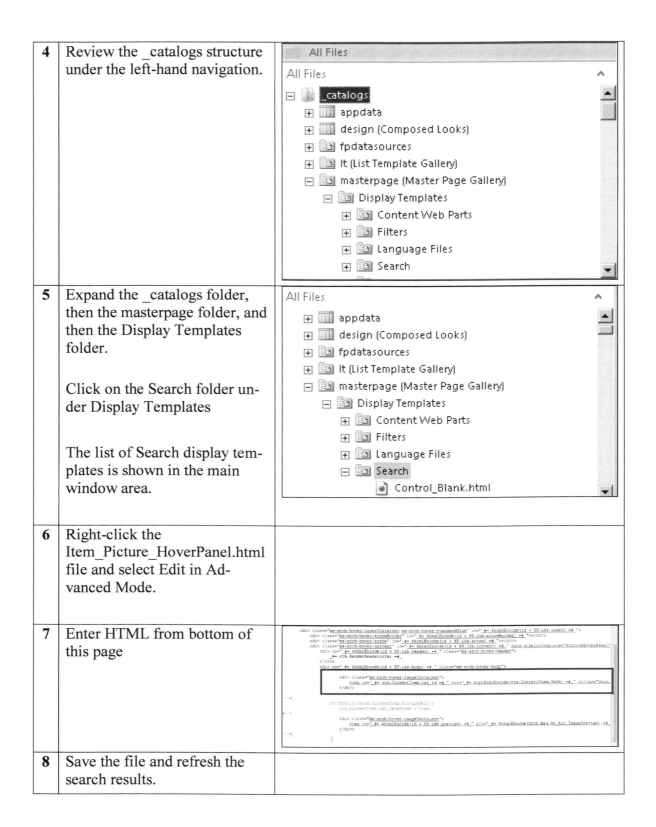
5	Expand the _catalogs folder, then the masterpage folder, and then the Display Templates folder. Click on the Search folder under Display Templates The list of Search display templates is shown in the main window area.	
6	Right-click the Item_Picture_HoverPanel.html file and select Edit in Advanced Mode.	
7	Enter HTML from bottom of this page	
8	Save the file and refresh the search results.	

```
<div class="ms-srch-hover-imageContainer">
<img id=" #= ctx.CurrentItem.csr_id =# " src=" #= $urlHtmlEncode(ctx.CurrentItem.Path) =# " on-
load="this.style.display='block';" />
</div>
```

A larger preview image shows in the hover now:

LAB 6

Installing and Configuring Office Web Apps Server

This lab walks through the installation and configuration of Office Web Apps Server integrated with SharePoint 2013.

Task 6-1A: Prepare for Office Web Apps Server on Windows Server 2008 R2

If you are using Windows Server 2008 R2, you need to make sure the following is installed first

- Windows Server 2008 R2 Service Pack 1
- .NET Framework 4.5
- Windows PowerShell 3.0
- KB2592525

Add the required server features using PowerShell

1	Launch PowerShell on the Server	
2	Enter `Import-Module ServerManager` Press Enter	
3	Run `Add-WindowsFeature Web-Server,Web-WebServer,Web-Common-Http,Web-Static-Content,Web-App-Dev,Web-Asp-Net,Web-Net-Ext,Web-ISAPI-Ext,Web-ISAPI-Filter,Web-Includes,Web-Security,Web-Windows-Auth,Web-Filtering,Web-Stat-Compression,Web-Dyn-Compression,Web-Mgmt-Console,Ink-Handwriting,IH-Ink-Support`	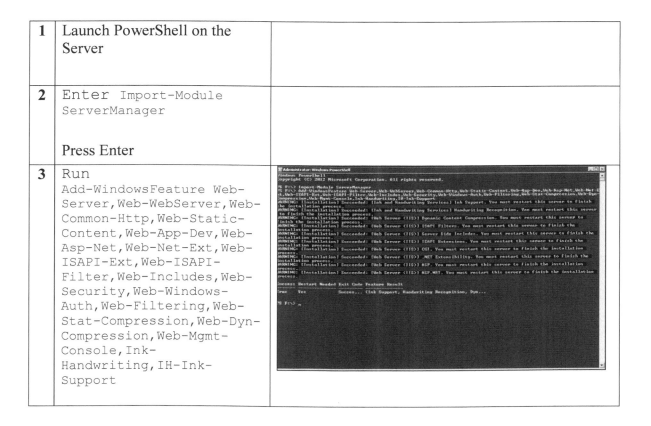

If the output shows that a restart is needed (Restart Needed = Yes), restart your server before continuing.

Task 6-1B: Prepare for Office Web Apps Server on Windows Server 2012

Preparing your server on Windows Server 2012 is slightly different. You need to add the features as follows

1	Launch PowerShell on the Server	
2	Enter `Import-Module ServerManager` **Press Enter**	
3	Run `Add-WindowsFeature Web-Server,Web-Mgmt-Tools,Web-Mgmt-Console,Web-WebServer,Web-Common-Http,Web-Default-Doc,Web-Static-Content,Web-Performance,Web-Stat-Compression,Web-Dyn-Compression,Web-Security,Web-Filtering,Web-Windows-Auth,Web-App-Dev,Web-Net-Ext45,Web-Asp-Net45,Web-ISAPI-Ext,Web-ISAPI-Filter,Web-In-cludes,InkandHandwritingServices`	

If the output shows that a restart is needed, restart your server before continuing.

Task 6-2: Download and Install Office Web Apps Server 2013 (October 2012 Release)

1	Download the Office Web Apps Server 2013 October 2013 Release	
2	Install Office Web Apps Server 2013 by double-clicking the **setup** application	

Task 6-3: Download and Install Office Web Apps Server 2013 Public Update (March 2013 Update)

1	Download the Office Web Apps Server 2013 Public Update	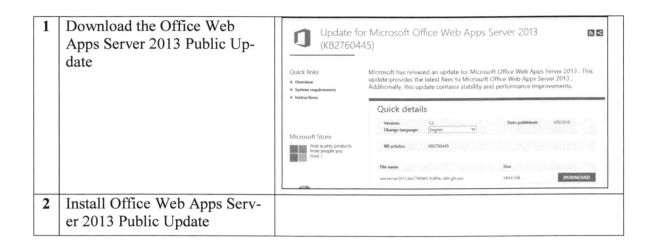
2	Install Office Web Apps Server 2013 Public Update	

Task 6-4: Create the Office Web Apps Farm

Now you need to create the new Office Web Apps Farm on the server via PowerShell

1	Launch PowerShell	
2	Enter `Import-Module OfficeWebApps` Press enter.	
3	Enter `New-OfficeWebAppsFarm -InternalURL http//servername -AllowHttp -EditingEnabled` `Press enter`	
4	Confirm the Editing operation	
5	Review results	
6	Test the Office Web Apps server using a browser to confirm that http//servername/hosting/discovery produces a wopi-discovery response	

Task 6-5: Bind SharePoint 2013 to Office Web Apps

1	On the SharePoint 2013 server, launch the SharePoint 2013 Management Shell	
2	Enter: New-SPWOPIBinding -ServerName <WacServerName> -AllowHTTP The bindings are shown.	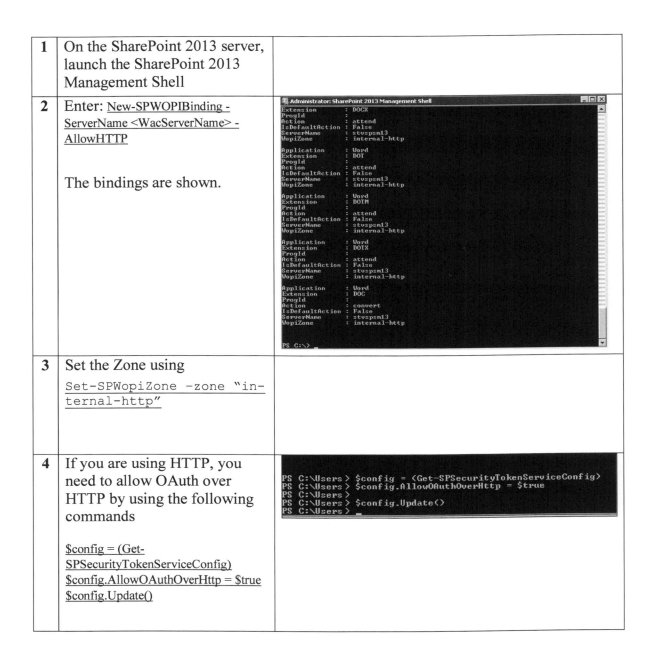
3	Set the Zone using `Set-SPWopiZone -zone "internal-http"`	
4	If you are using HTTP, you need to allow OAuth over HTTP by using the following commands $config = (Get-SPSecurityTokenServiceConfig) $config.AllowOAuthOverHttp = $true $config.Update()	

Task 6-6: Verify SharePoint 2013 is Using Office Web Apps

1	Browse a document library with Office documents	
2	Click on the ellipsis to see the preview	
3	Navigate to your search center and search for Office documents (you may need to perform a full crawl before the preview kicks in)	
4	Hover over an Office document result and verify the preview	

LAB 7

Handling PDF Documents

This lab walks through the configuration and behaviors of PDF documents.

PDF Handling Overview

SharePoint 2013 supports PDF documents out-of-the-box. Initially, web applications do not allow opening PDFs in the browser, however, by adding PDF as an allowed MIME type, browser rendering via Adobe is achieved.

Office Web Apps server provides Office document previews and rendering in Search results without the need for client applications installed (e.g. Word, Excel, etc.). However, once SharePoint is bound to Office Web Apps, PDF documents no longer open in the browser.

There are two workarounds –

1) Configure PDF items to render as Word Items which allows PDFs to open and preview in Search within Office Web Apps

2) Modify the PDF Item display template which allows PDFs to render in the browser via Adobe. Modify the PDF hover template to display previews.

These workarounds take care of Search, but PDFs will still open in the client application (e.g. Adobe) from Document Libraries. The solution here is an update to Office Web Apps. The February/March 2013 Update to Office Web Apps server supports opening PDFs from document libraries within Office Web Apps.

The following table summarizes the various PDF rendering and preview behaviors:

	Search PDF Preview	Search Open (clicking on result)	Document Library Open (clicking on Document)
Out of the Box (Strict Web App)	Available by modifying the Display Template	Opens in Adobe or associated client application	Opens in Adobe or associated client application
Out of the Box (Permissive Web App or Allowed Mime Type of PDF)	Available by modifying the Display Template	Opens in web browser and search term is passed into Adobe	Web Browser
Office Web Apps Server (October 2012 Release)	Two options: 1. Display template (shows in Adobe web) 2. Modify Result Type to use Word Item (shows in Word App Web)	Opens in Adobe or associated client application. Opens in Browser with modification of display template	Opens in Adobe or associated client application.
Office Web Apps Server (Feb/Mar 2013 Update)	Two options: 1. Display template (shows in Adobe web) 2. Modify Result Type to use Word Item (shows in Word App Web)	Opens in browser using Word Web App Can use templates to display in Adobe Web.	Opens in browser using Word Web App If not bound to WordPDF – Opens in Adobe or associated client application.

It is also worth mentioning that if Office Web Apps is not used for Search results of PDFs, the opening of PDFs in the browser passes the search terms into Adobe and thus finds the occurrences within the document. An example of this "search term pass-through" is displayed below

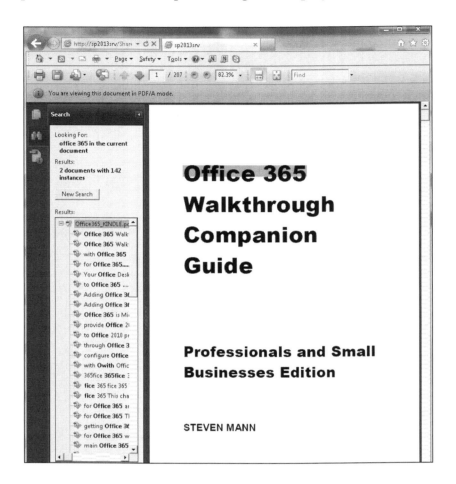

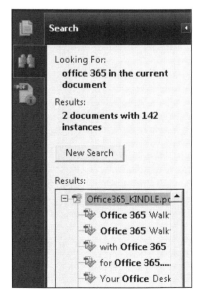

When using Office Web Apps server with SharePoint, there are two overall options when handling PDFs. One provides a more consistent user experience and the other provides the most functionality.

Most Consistent User Experience

The most consistent user experience would be to use Office Web Apps server (with the update) to enable opening of PDFs from libraries in the browser and to modify the search result type to render PDFs as Word Items which enables both preview and opening of the documents from Search results within Office Web Apps.

Most Functionality

The option that provides the most functionality is to use Office Web Apps for document libraries such that PDFs are opened within the browser but then use customized search templates to preview and open PDFs from Search results thus providing the search term pass-through functionality as described above. For the most consistent preview, use a customized copy of the Word item hover panel template.

Task 7-1: PDF Preview by Modifying Display Templates

This method of PDF previews involves the modification of search display templates.

1	Fire up SharePoint Designer 2013 and Open the Search Center Site	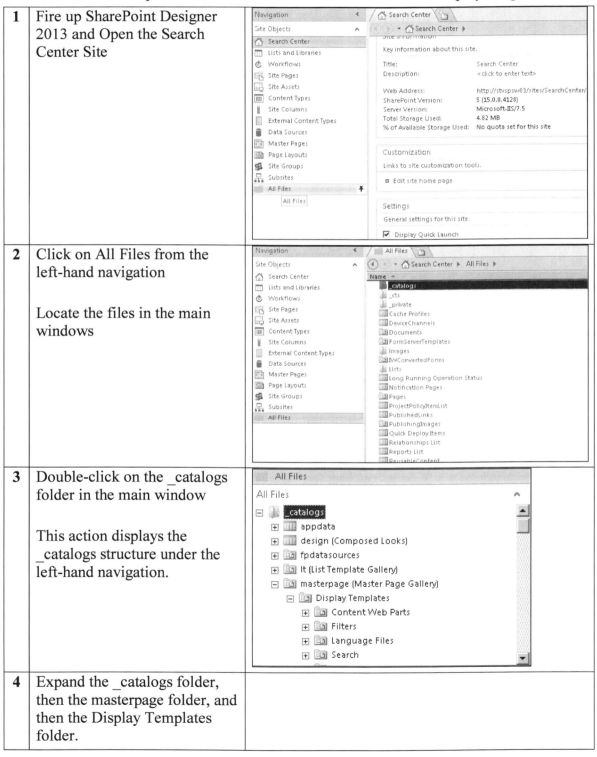
2	Click on All Files from the left-hand navigation Locate the files in the main windows	
3	Double-click on the _catalogs folder in the main window This action displays the _catalogs structure under the left-hand navigation.	
4	Expand the _catalogs folder, then the masterpage folder, and then the Display Templates folder.	

5	Click on the Search folder under Display Templates The list of Search display templates is shown in the main window area.	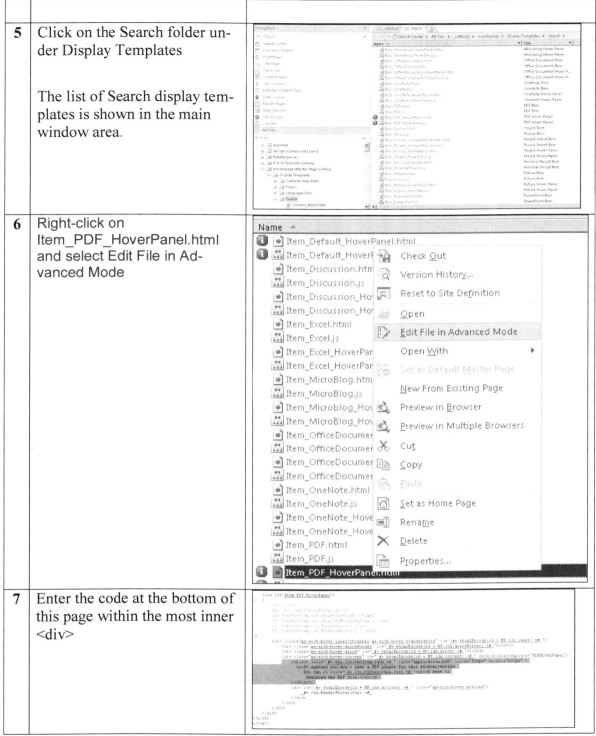
6	Right-click on Item_PDF_HoverPanel.html and select Edit File in Advanced Mode	
7	Enter the code at the bottom of this page within the most inner <div>	

```
<object data="  #= ctx.CurrentItem.Path =#  " type="application/pdf" width="100%" height="500px" >
<p>It appears you don't have a PDF plugin for this browser/device.
You can <a href="  #= ctx.CurrentItem.Path =#  ">click here to
download the PDF file.</a></p>
</object>
```

7	Save the file . When saving the file, you may get a warning about breaking from the site definition. Click OK. Behind the scenes the HTML changes are incorporated into the javascript version of the template (Item_PDF_HoverPanel.js).	
8	Perform a search from your search center that produces PDF document results. Hover over the PDF document to see the preview	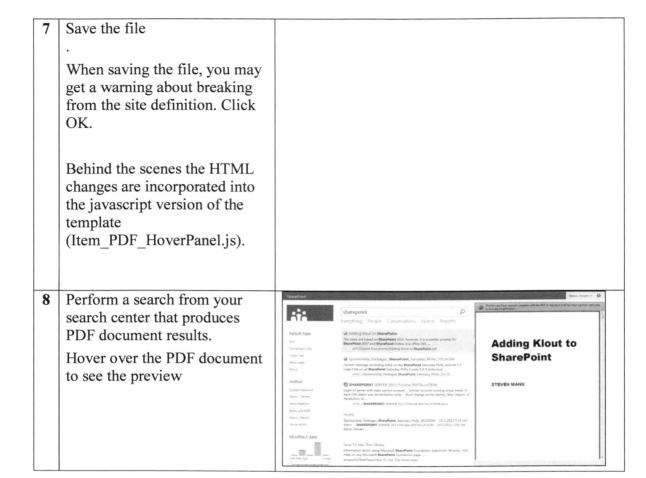

Task 7-2: PDF Preview by Copying Result Type (using Office Web Apps Server)

When using Office Web Apps Server with SharePoint 2013, there is an easier way to present PDF previews without having to modify the search display templates. This involves copying and modifying the PDF result type and have it render as a Word Item.

1	The first step is to navigate to your Search Center site settings	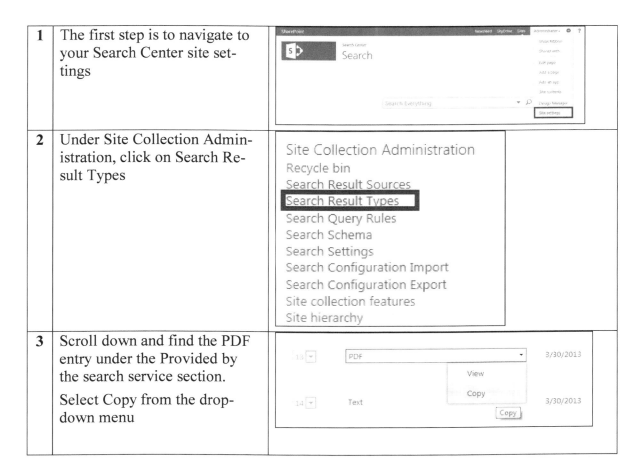
2	Under Site Collection Administration, click on Search Result Types	
3	Scroll down and find the PDF entry under the Provided by the search service section. Select Copy from the drop-down menu	

4	On the Add Result Type page, rename the item and select Word Item under "What should these results look like"	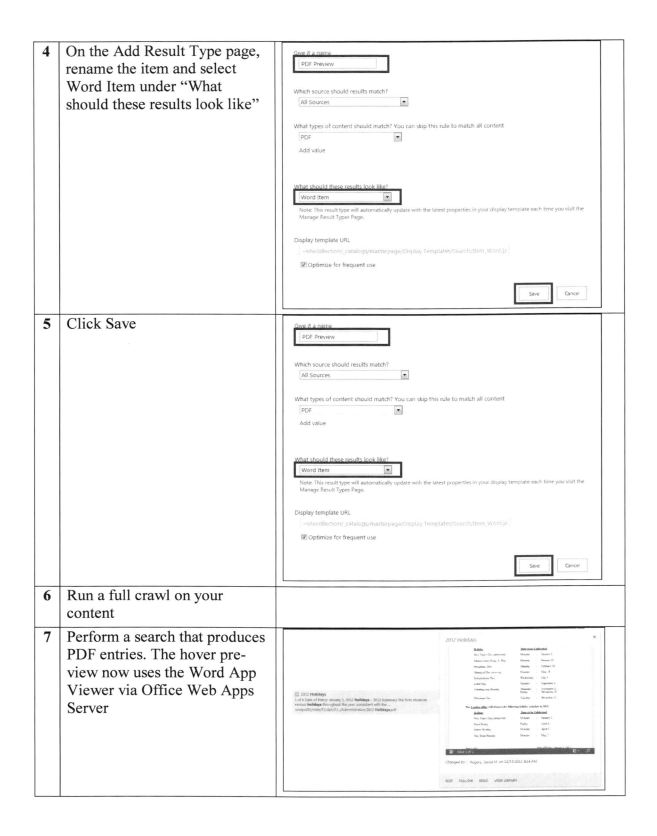
5	Click Save	
6	Run a full crawl on your content	
7	Perform a search that produces PDF entries. The hover pre-view now uses the Word App Viewer via Office Web Apps Server	

Adding People to Everything Results

This lab demonstrates the use of Promoted Block Results to add People to the Everything Results page.

Once again, the main search results, which is now called Everything, does not include People search results. So it's not really everything. The reason is because there is a special People Search Results web
part that is catered towards the User Profiles and their respective properties. With SharePoint 2013
Search capabilities, you may add people results into your main search (Everything). This lab walks you
through the steps.

1	Go to the site settings of your Search Center and under Site Collection Administration click on Search Query Rules	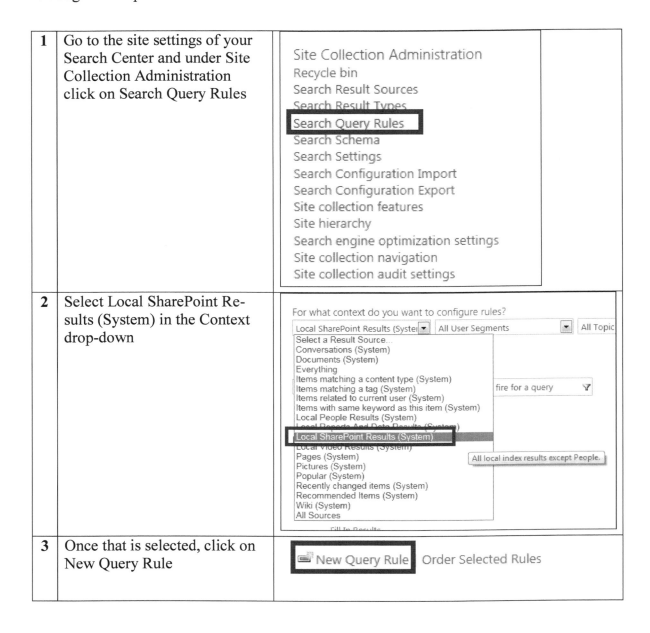
2	Select Local SharePoint Results (System) in the Context drop-down	
3	Once that is selected, click on New Query Rule	

4	On the Add Query Rule page, add a rule name, remove the condition, and then click on the Add Result Block link	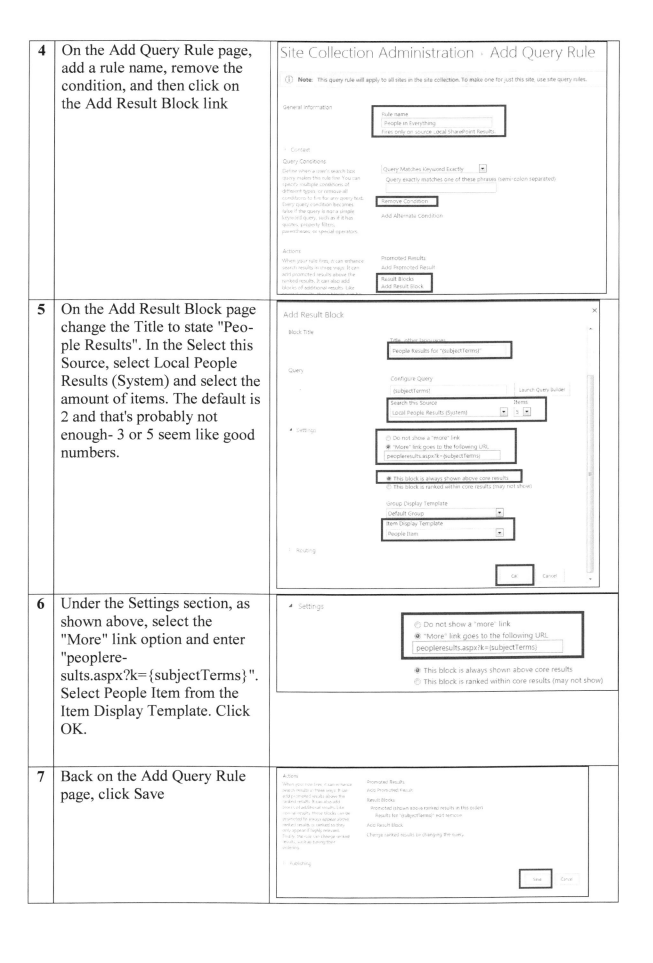
5	On the Add Result Block page change the Title to state "People Results". In the Select this Source, select Local People Results (System) and select the amount of items. The default is 2 and that's probably not enough- 3 or 5 seem like good numbers.	
6	Under the Settings section, as shown above, select the "More" link option and enter "peopleresults.aspx?k={subjectTerms}". Select People Item from the Item Display Template. Click OK.	
7	Back on the Add Query Rule page, click Save	

| 8 | Run your search query again (it may take a moment for the changes to appear)

Now you have people results appearing in the search results under Everything! |  |

Adding a Custom Result Type Based on Location of Documents

This lab demonstrates the creation of a custom result type using the query builder to define the items to include. The scenario is that Human Resources (HR) produces and maintains policy documents in PDF format. These documents are stored all within a particular location on the HR department site. Users need to be able to search within Policies and have the appropriate results display. Creating a new search results page and adding it to the search navigation is also

Task 9-1: Create a Custom Result Source

1	Navigate to your Search Center and select Site Settings from the Settings menu	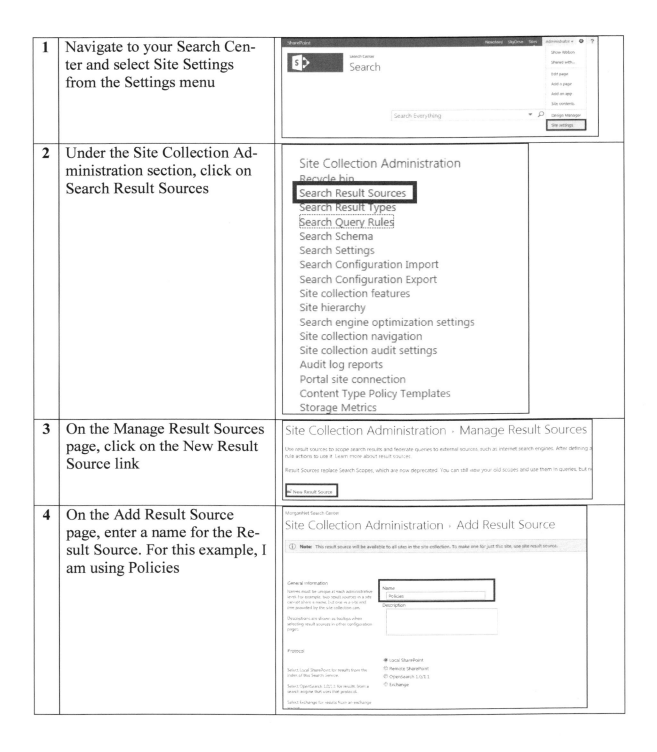
2	Under the Site Collection Administration section, click on Search Result Sources	
3	On the Manage Result Sources page, click on the New Result Source link	
4	On the Add Result Source page, enter a name for the Result Source. For this example, I am using Policies	

5	Scroll down and click on the Launch Query Builder button	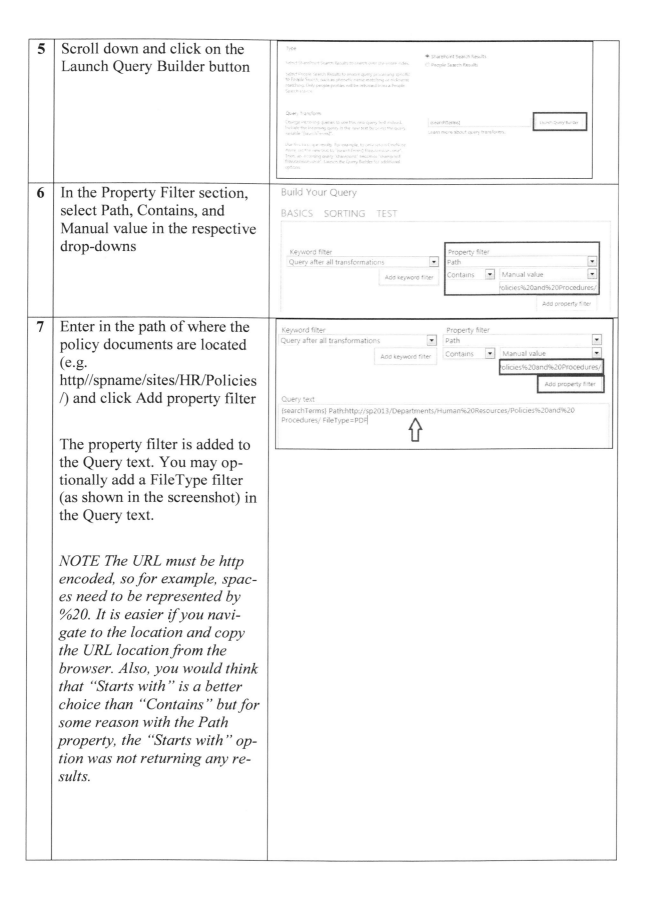
6	In the Property Filter section, select Path, Contains, and Manual value in the respective drop-downs	
7	Enter in the path of where the policy documents are located (e.g. http//spname/sites/HR/Policies/) and click Add property filter The property filter is added to the Query text. You may optionally add a FileType filter (as shown in the screenshot) in the Query text. *NOTE The URL must be http encoded, so for example, spaces need to be represented by %20. It is easier if you navigate to the location and copy the URL location from the browser. Also, you would think that "Starts with" is a better choice than "Contains" but for some reason with the Path property, the "Starts with" option was not returning any results.*	

8	Click OK on the Build Your Query dialog. The property filter is added to the Query Transform text box.	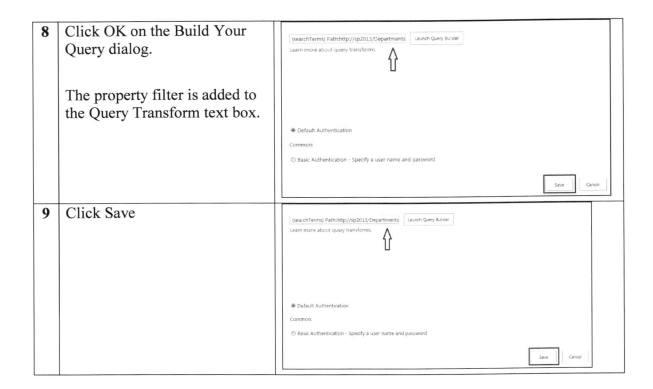
9	Click Save	

Task 9-2: Create a Custom Result Type for the Custom Result Source

1	Navigate to your Search Center and select Site Settings from the Settings menu. Under the Site Collection Administration section, click on the Search Result Types link	Site Collection Administration Recycle bin Search Result Sources Search Result Types Search Query Rules Search Schema Search Settings Search Configuration Import Search Configuration Export Site collection features Site hierarchy Search engine optimization settings Site collection navigation
2	On the Result Types page click on the New Result Type link	Search Center Site Collection Administration Tailor the look of important result types by crafting a display template in HTML and defining a rule that priority. Learn more about how to configure result types New Result Type
3	Enter a name for the Result Type. Select the Result Source created in the previous task section from the source drop-down. In this example, all Policy documents are PDF so the content and display templates are the PDF options	Give it a name Policy Which source should results match? Policies What types of content should match? You can skip this rule to match all content PDF Add value What should these results look like? PDF Item Note: This result type will automatically update with the latest properties in your display template each time you visit the Manage Result Types Page. Display template URL ~sitecollection/_catalogs/masterpage/display templates/search/Item_PDF.js Optimize for frequent use Save Cancel
4	Click Save	

Task 9-3: Create a Custom Results Page for the Custom Result Type

1	Navigate to your Search Center and select Site Contents from the Settings menu	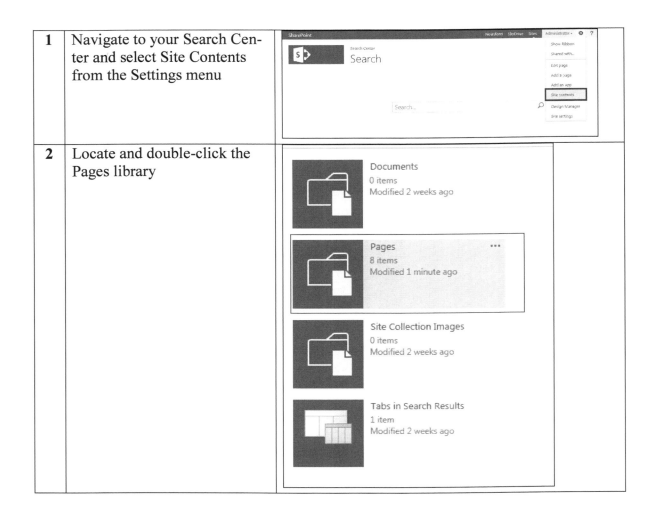
2	Locate and double-click the Pages library	

3	From the Files tab in the top ribbon, select Page from the New Document drop-down menu	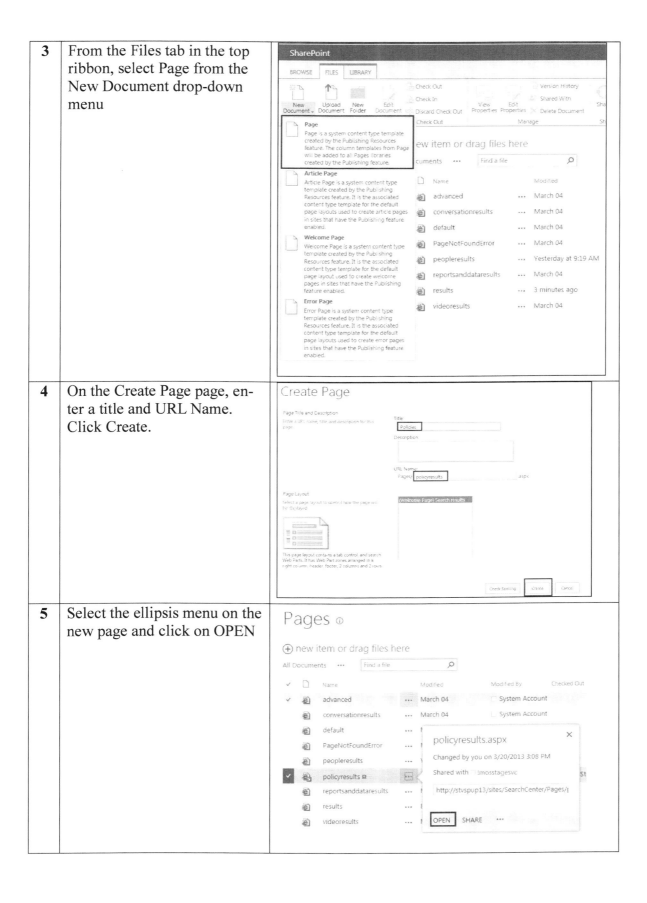
4	On the Create Page page, enter a title and URL Name. Click Create.	
5	Select the ellipsis menu on the new page and click on OPEN	

6	From the Settings menu select Edit page	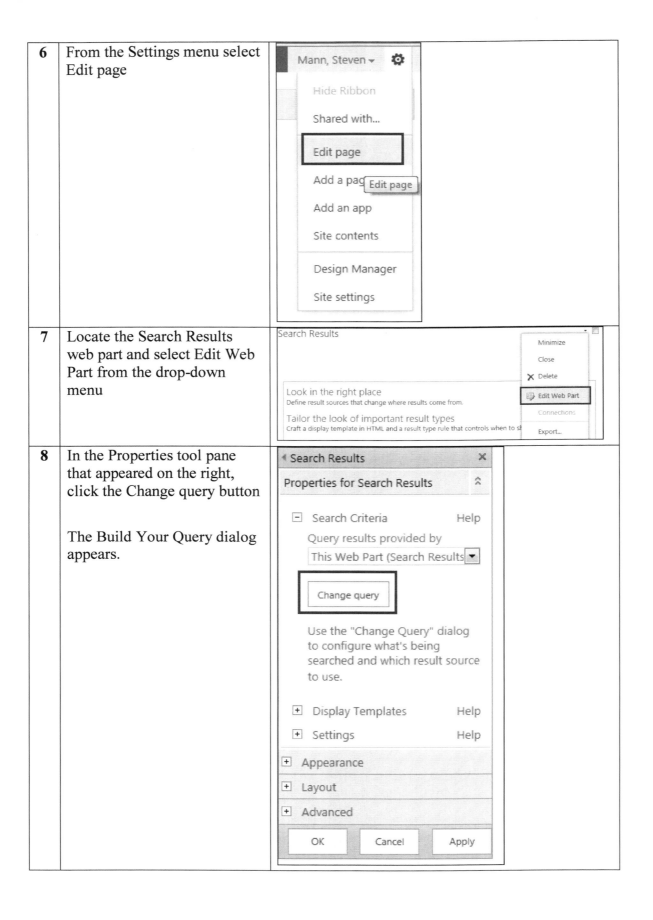
7	Locate the Search Results web part and select Edit Web Part from the drop-down menu	
8	In the Properties tool pane that appeared on the right, click the Change query button The Build Your Query dialog appears.	

9	In the Select a query section, select the custom Result Source created in the first task of this lab	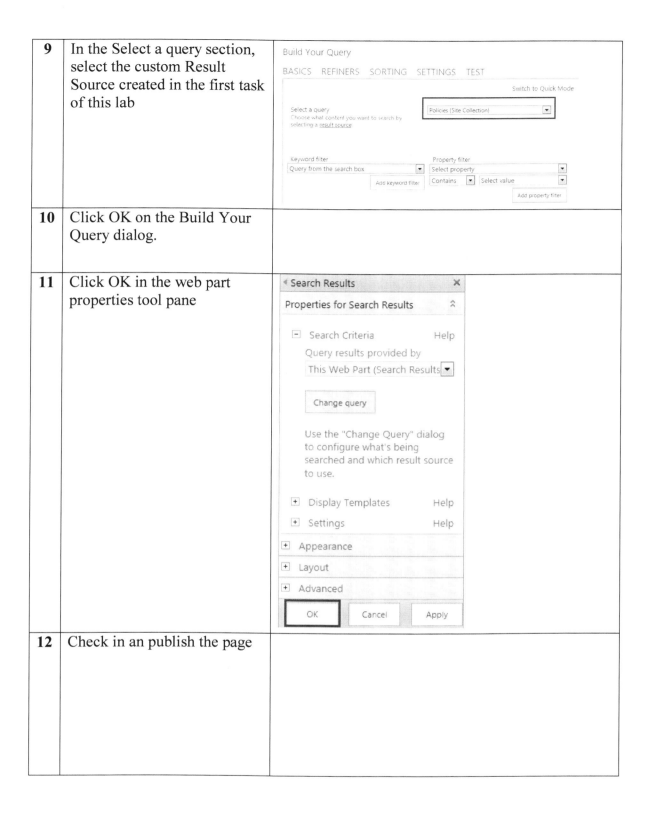
10	Click OK on the Build Your Query dialog.	
11	Click OK in the web part properties tool pane	
12	Check in an publish the page	

Task 9-4: Add a Custom Results Page to the Search Center Navigation

1	Navigate to your Search Center and select Site Settings from the Settings menu	
2	Under the Search section click the Search Settings link	
3	At the bottom the Search Settings page, click on Add Link…	
4	Enter a title and the URL to the custom page that was created in the previous task section. Click OK.	

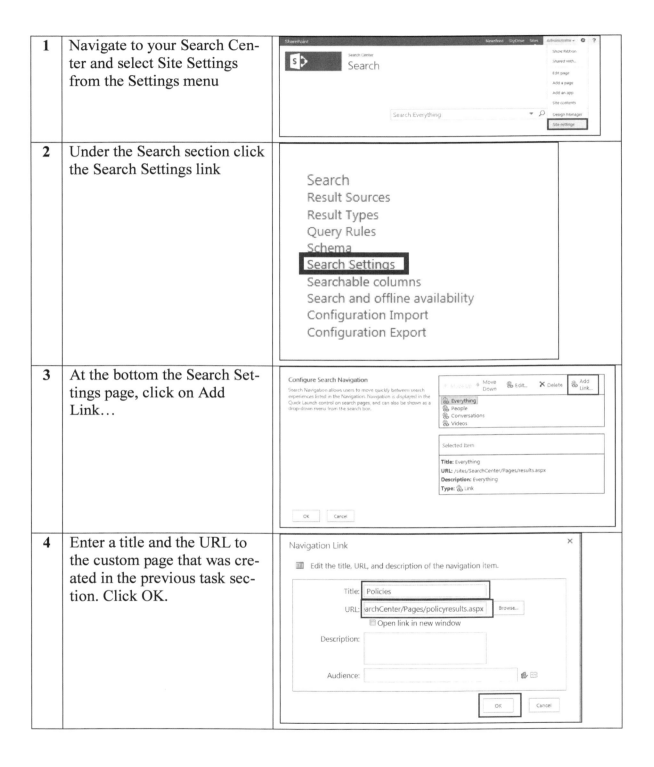

| 5 | Back on the Search Settings page click OK | 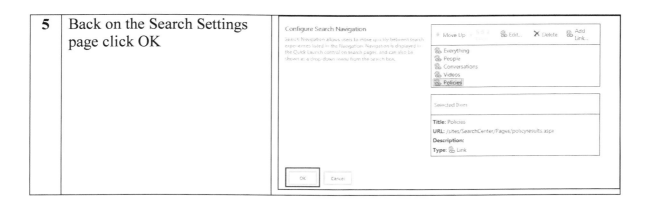 |

Task 9-5: Test the Results

| 1 | Navigate to your Search Center. The new navigation item appears at the top. Click on the new link and perform a search | holidays   🔍

 Everything   People   Videos   Policies

 📄 **Holidays** - 2012 <br> office will observe the following **holiday** schedule in 2012:
 Holiday Date to be Celebrated New Year **Holidays** Monday - January 2 Tuesday - January 3Page 6 of 8 ...
 /Departments/.../Attendance and Leaves/**Holidays** - 2012.pdf

 📄 Table of Contents
 Bereavement ⬜ Family and Medical Leave ⬜ **Holidays** ⬜ Jury Duty and Witness
 /Departments/.../Document Library/Table of Contents.pdf

 📄 Late Hours-Meal and Transportation Reimbursement - Administr...
 No meal expense is paid to ... 3. Reimbursement On Weekends and **Holidays**
 /.../Late Hours-Meal and Transportation Reimbursement - Ad... |

Promoting Results

This lab demonstrates the promotion of particular results as well as promoted results blocks. The examples here build on top of the Policies result type produced in Lab 9.

Task 10-1: Add a Promoted Result to Everything Results

From the previous Lab, you now have a Policies search and results in the navigation. However, if some-one searches for a policy in Everything, you want to make sure particular results are shown at the top. In this case, when someone searches for "holidays", you want to display the Holiday policy document first. This task explains those steps.

1	Navigate to your Search Center and select Site Settings from the Settings menu	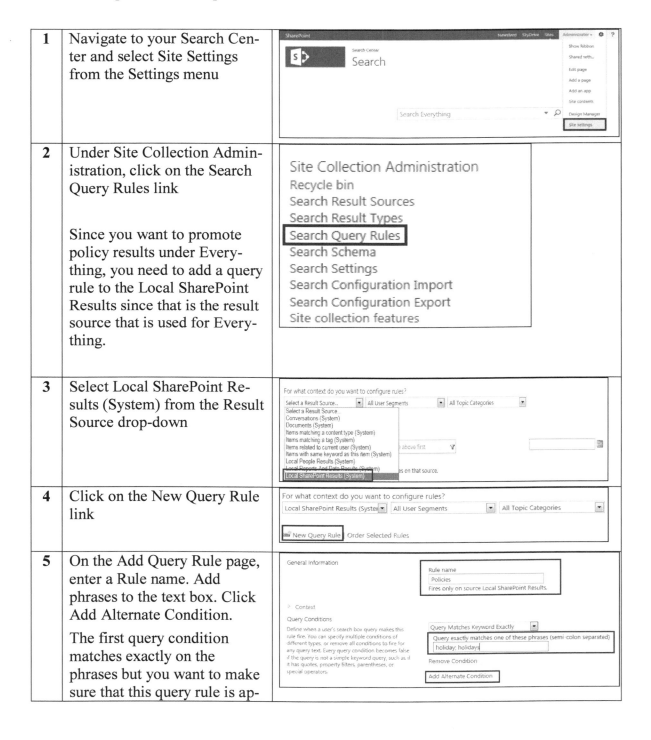
2	Under Site Collection Administration, click on the Search Query Rules link

Since you want to promote policy results under Everything, you need to add a query rule to the Local SharePoint Results since that is the result source that is used for Everything. | |
| 3 | Select Local SharePoint Results (System) from the Result Source drop-down | |
| 4 | Click on the New Query Rule link | |
| 5 | On the Add Query Rule page, enter a Rule name. Add phrases to the text box. Click Add Alternate Condition.

The first query condition matches exactly on the phrases but you want to make sure that this query rule is ap- | |

	plied if the search contains any of the phrases as well.	
6	In the second query condition, select Query Contains Action Term and then enter the same phrases into the text box	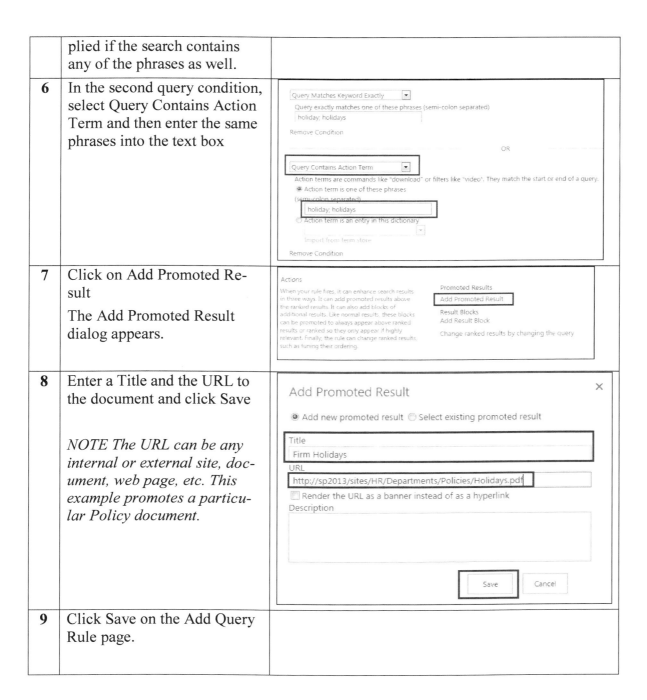
7	Click on Add Promoted Result The Add Promoted Result dialog appears.	
8	Enter a Title and the URL to the document and click Save *NOTE The URL can be any internal or external site, document, web page, etc. This example promotes a particular Policy document.*	
9	Click Save on the Add Query Rule page.	

Task 10-2: Test a Promoted Result

1	Navigate back to your Search center and enter a search term that matches the query rule from the previous task. The promoted result is displayed at the top of the results with a blue check mark next to it.	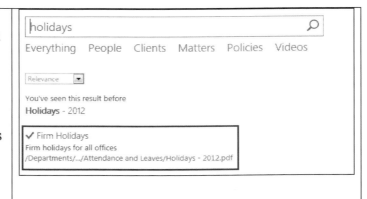

Task 10-3: Expand a Promoted Result to Include a Promoted Result Block

1	Navigate to your Search Center and select Site Settings from the Settings menu	
2	Under Site Collection Administration, click on the Search Query Rules link	
3	Select Local SharePoint Results (System) from the Result Source drop-down	
4	Find the query rule created from the previous tasks and select Edit from the drop-down	
5	At the bottom of the Query Rule page, click on Add Result Block	

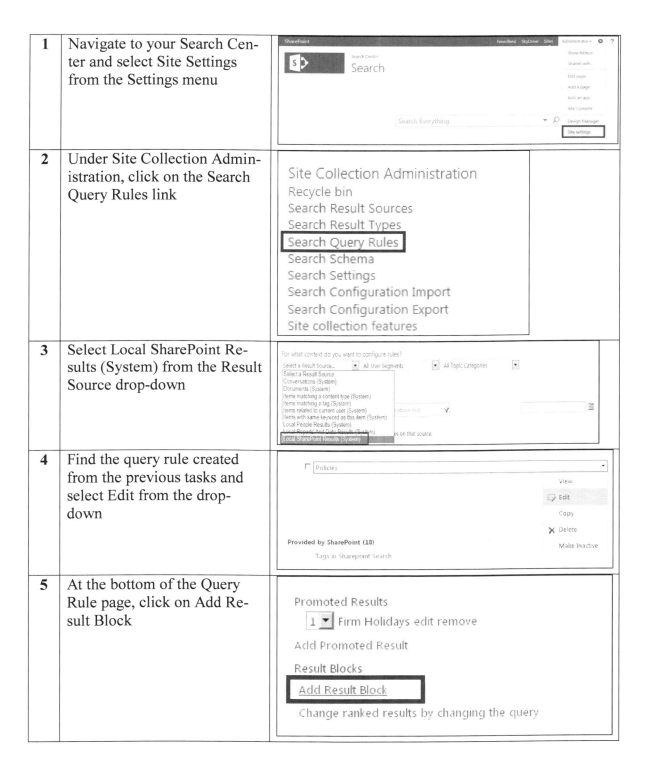

6	Fill out the Result Block details (similar to adding Everything to People) Click OK.	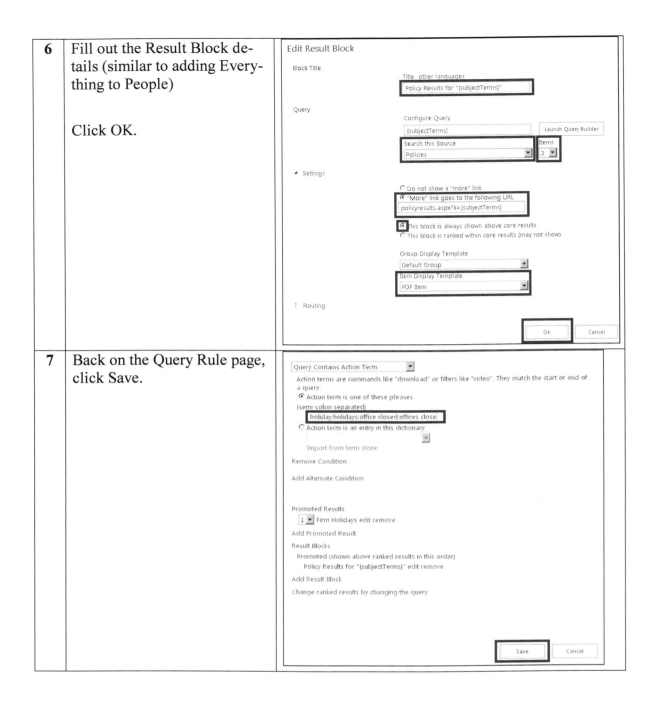
7	Back on the Query Rule page, click Save.	

Task 10-4: Test Results from a Promoted Result Block

1	Navigate back to your Search Center and enter terms that match your query rule Now both a promoted result and a promoted result block appear when the search terms match the query rule.	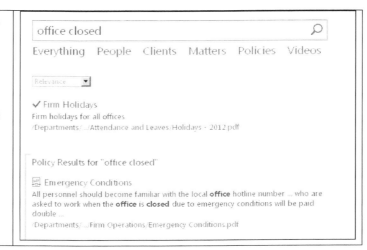

The image content (search results):

office closed

Everything   People   Clients   Matters   Policies   Videos

Relevance

✓ Firm Holidays
Firm holidays for all offices
/Departments/.../Attendance and Leaves/Holidays - 2012.pdf

Policy Results for "office closed"

Emergency Conditions
All personnel should become familiar with the local **office** hotline number ... who are asked to work when the **office** is **closed** due to emergency conditions will be paid double ...
/Departments/.../Firm Operations/Emergency Conditions.pdf

Incorporating External Data using BCS and External Content Types

This lab demonstrates an end-to-end solution incorporating customer data into your Search Center experience. The Business Data Connectivity Service is used to produce an external content type based on a customer database.

Task 11-1: Prepare the Data Source

The scenario and sample data for this lab uses Product information from the AdventureWorks2012 sample database in SQL Server.

1	The first step is to create your read list and read item procedures. Create a stored procedure that returns all of the information you want to search and make sure all rows are returned	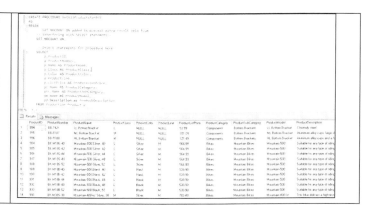

```
CREATE PROCEDURE GetAllProductsForBCS
AS
BEGIN
        -- SET NOCOUNT ON added to prevent extra result sets from
        -- interfering with SELECT statements.
        SET NOCOUNT ON;

    -- Insert statements for procedure here
        SELECT
                p.ProductID,
                p.ProductNumber,
                p.Name AS ProductName,
                p.Class AS ProductClass,
                p.Color AS ProductColor,
                p.ProductLine,
                p.ListPrice AS ProductListPrice,
                pc.Name AS ProductCategory,
                psc.Name AS ProductSubCategory,
                pm.Name AS ProductModel,
                pd.Description as ProductDescription
        FROM Production.Product p
                INNER JOIN Production.ProductSubcategory psc
                        ON psc.ProductSubcategoryID = p.ProductSubcategoryID
                INNER JOIN Production.ProductCategory pc
                        ON pc.ProductCategoryID = psc.ProductCategoryID
                INNER JOIN Production.ProductModel pm
                        on pm.ProductModelID = p.ProductModelID
                INNER JOIN Production.ProductModelProductDescriptionCulture pmx
                        ON pm.ProductModelID = pmx.ProductModelID
                INNER JOIN Production.ProductDescription pd
                        ON pmx.ProductDescriptionID = pd.ProductDescriptionID
        WHERE pmx.CultureID='en'
```

This procedure is used to create a ReadList method in the External Content Type.

2	Create a stored procedure that returns the same information but only for a particular entity by using the ID as a parameter Make sure only 1 row is returned for a given identity.	

```
CREATE PROCEDURE GetProductByProductIDForBCS (@ProductID INT)
AS
BEGIN
        -- SET NOCOUNT ON added to prevent extra result sets from
        -- interfering with SELECT statements.
        SET NOCOUNT ON;

    -- Insert statements for procedure here
        SELECT
                p.ProductID,
                p.ProductNumber,
                p.Name AS ProductName,
                p.Class AS ProductClass,
                p.Color AS ProductColor,
                p.ProductLine,
                p.ListPrice AS ProductListPrice,
                pc.Name AS ProductCategory,
                psc.Name AS ProductSubCategory,
                pm.Name AS ProductModel,
                pd.Description as ProductDescription
        FROM Production.Product p
            INNER JOIN Production.ProductSubcategory psc
                    ON psc.ProductSubcategoryID = p.ProductSubcategoryID
            INNER JOIN Production.ProductCategory pc
                    ON pc.ProductCategoryID = psc.ProductCategoryID
            INNER JOIN Production.ProductModel pm
                on pm.ProductModelID = p.ProductModelID
             INNER JOIN Production.ProductModelProductDescriptionCulture pmx
                    ON pm.ProductModelID = pmx.ProductModelID
            INNER JOIN Production.ProductDescription pd
                    ON pmx.ProductDescriptionID = pd.ProductDescriptionID
        WHERE p.ProductID = @ProductID
            AND pmx.CultureID='en'
```

This procedure is used to create a ReadItem method in the External Content Type. The SELECT statement here should be exactly the same as the SELECT in the ReadList. The only difference here is that additional WHERE condition for the passed in @ProductID.

Task 11-2: Add Credentials to the Secure Store Service

In order for the External Content Type to be created and BCS to access your external data source, the data source credentials need to be stored. The Secure Store Service in SharePoint allows you to store credentials. For this scenario, a SQL database account was created named "AWDBAccount". Therefore an entry in the Secure Store Service needs to be added for SQL Authentication.

1	Navigate to Central Administration and click on Manage Service Applications under the Application Management section	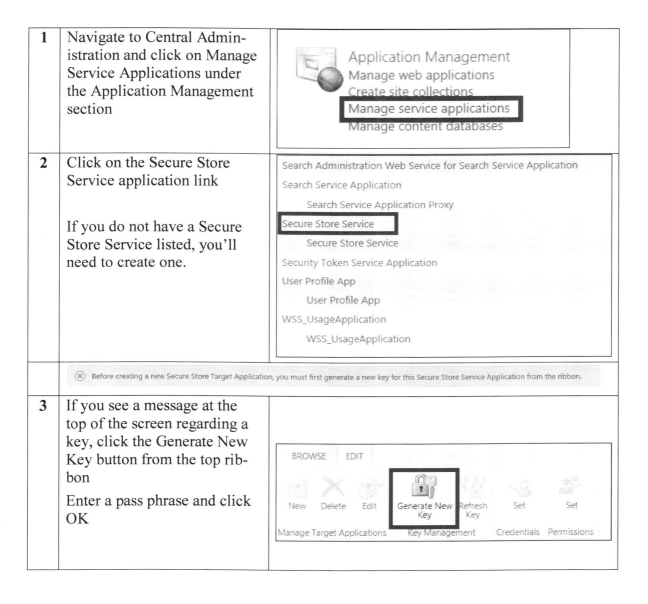
2	Click on the Secure Store Service application link If you do not have a Secure Store Service listed, you'll need to create one.	
3	If you see a message at the top of the screen regarding a key, click the Generate New Key button from the top ribbon Enter a pass phrase and click OK	

		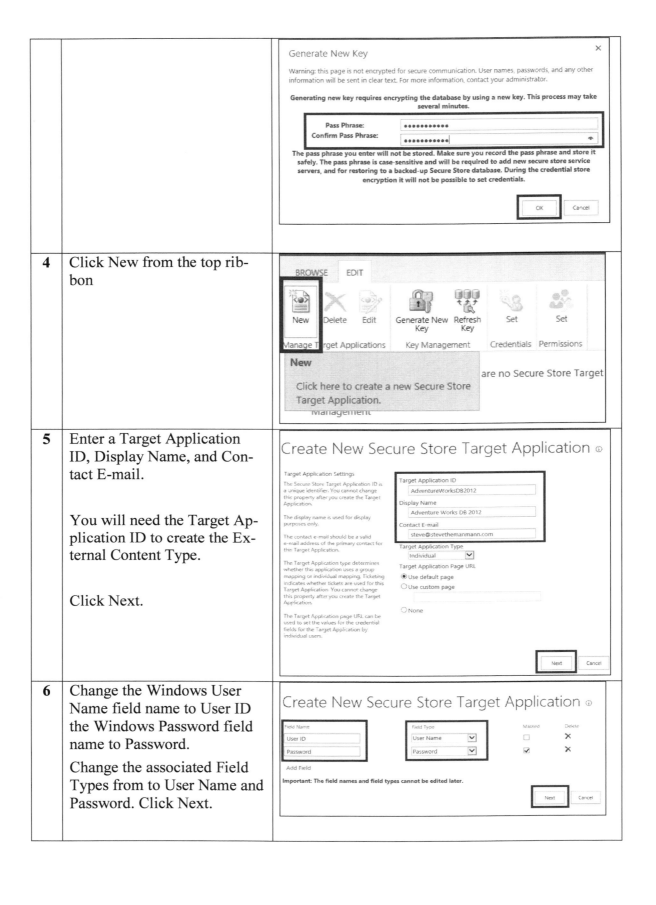
4	Click New from the top ribbon	
5	Enter a Target Application ID, Display Name, and Contact E-mail. You will need the Target Application ID to create the External Content Type. Click Next.	
6	Change the Windows User Name field name to User ID the Windows Password field name to Password. Change the associated Field Types from to User Name and Password. Click Next.	

7	Enter Target Application Administrators and click OK The Target Application entry is created	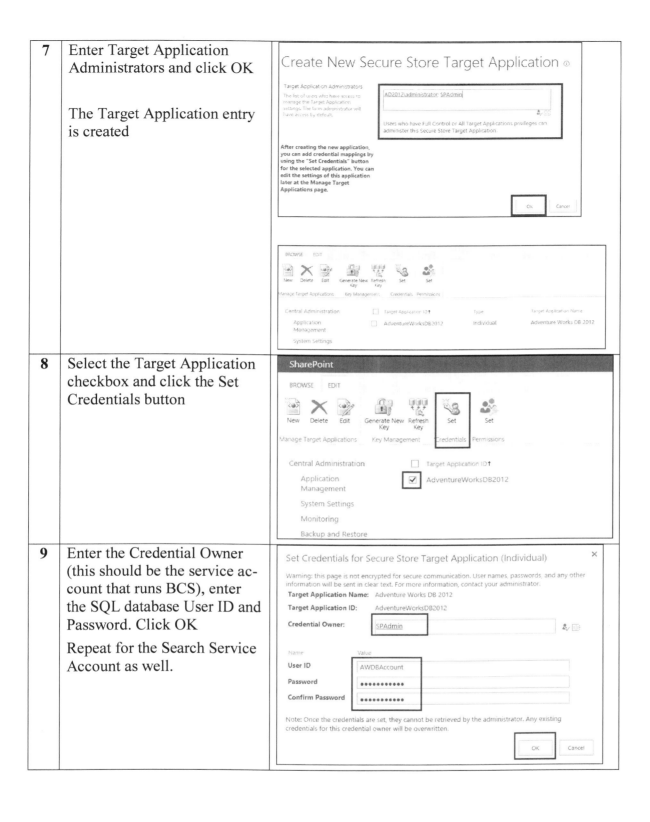
8	Select the Target Application checkbox and click the Set Credentials button	
9	Enter the Credential Owner (this should be the service account that runs BCS), enter the SQL database User ID and Password. Click OK Repeat for the Search Service Account as well.	

Task 11-3: Create an External Content Type

The methods here describe the steps for a no-code solution in creating an External Content Type that uses your data source as the provider of information via SharePoint Designer 2013.

| 1 | Launch SharePoint Designer 2013 and open your Search Center site | 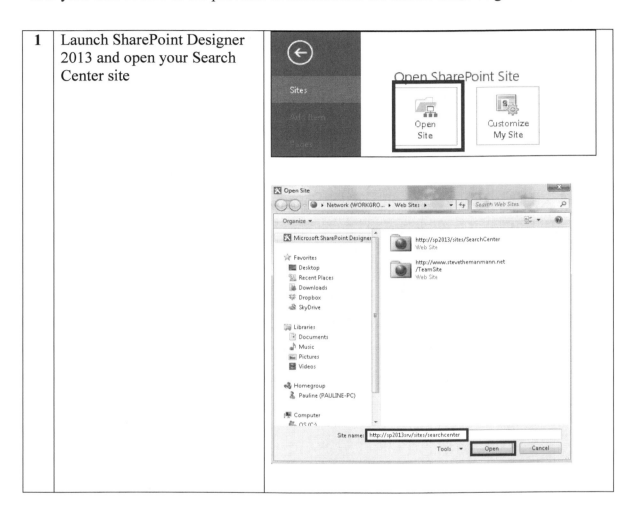 |

2	Click the External Content Types from the Site Objects and then click the External Content Type button from the top-ribbon	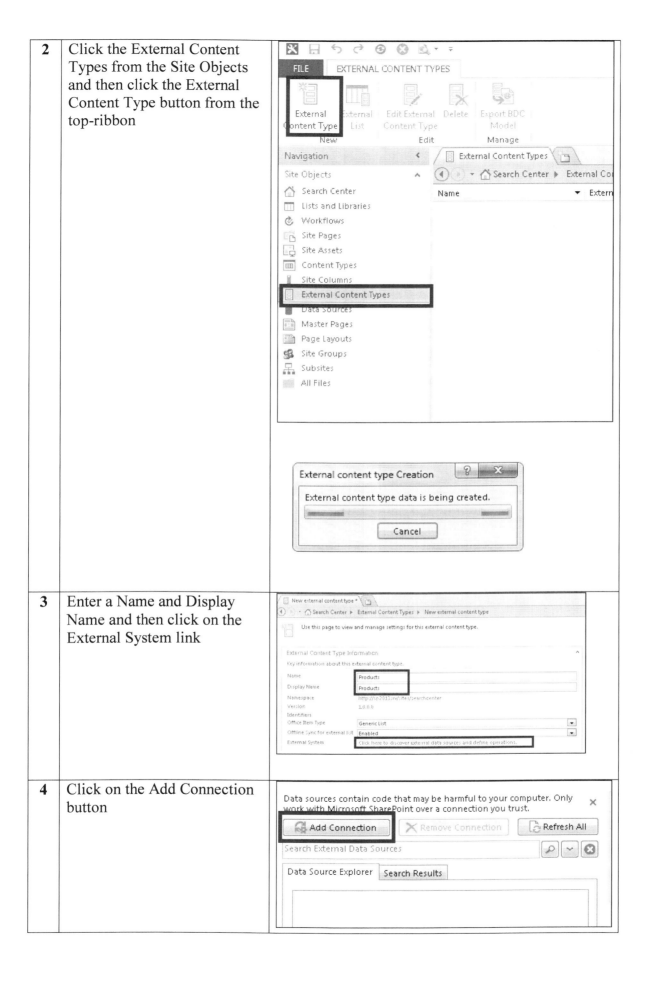
3	Enter a Name and Display Name and then click on the External System link	
4	Click on the Add Connection button	

5	Select the type of connection. For this lab, SQL Server is being used. Click OK.	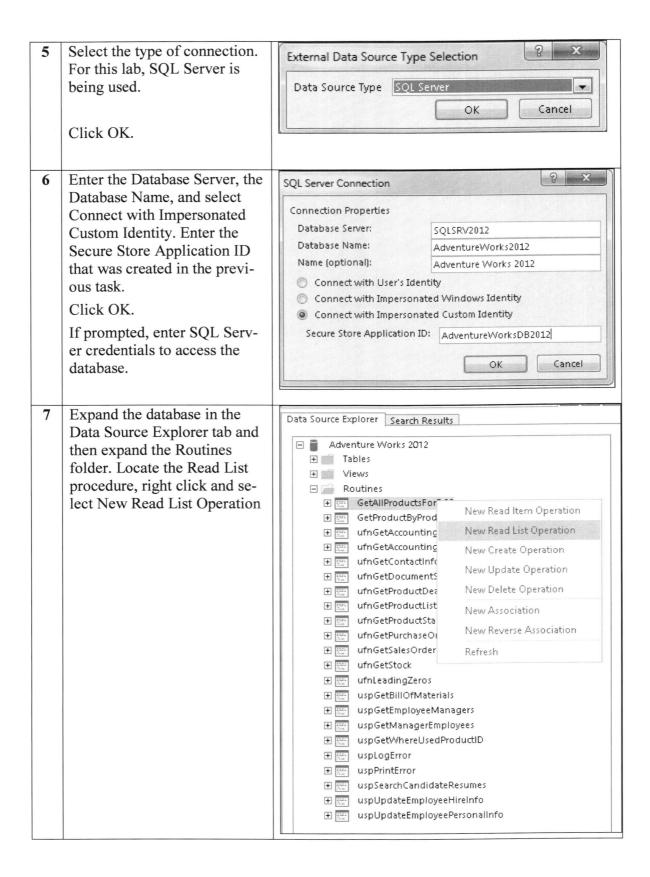
6	Enter the Database Server, the Database Name, and select Connect with Impersonated Custom Identity. Enter the Secure Store Application ID that was created in the previous task. Click OK. If prompted, enter SQL Server credentials to access the database.	
7	Expand the database in the Data Source Explorer tab and then expand the Routines folder. Locate the Read List procedure, right click and select New Read List Operation	

8	Enter an Operation Name and Display Name. The Operation Name becomes a prefix (ReadList.propertyname) in the crawled properties so it is a good idea to include an entity description in the name, otherwise it would be hard to distinguish crawled properties from their external content types. Click Next.	
9	The example does not limit the Read List items and thus there are no Input Parameters. Click Next	
10	On the Return Parameter Configuration screen, make sure the row identifier (primary key) is selected and check the Map to Identifier checkbox. The Identifier, Field, and DisplayName become populated with the row identifier. Click Finish.	

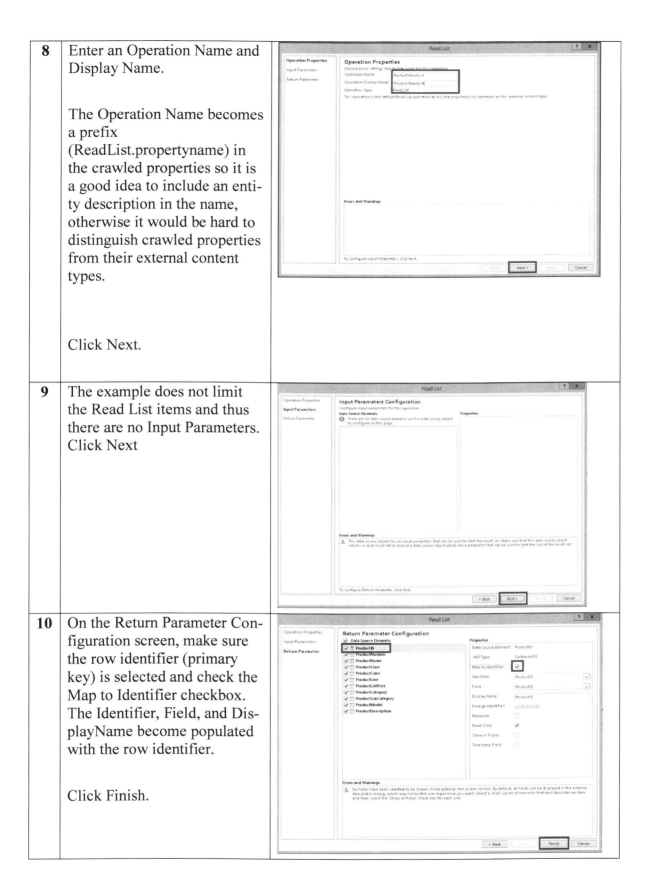

11	Next, locate the Read Item procedure, right click and select New Read Item Operation	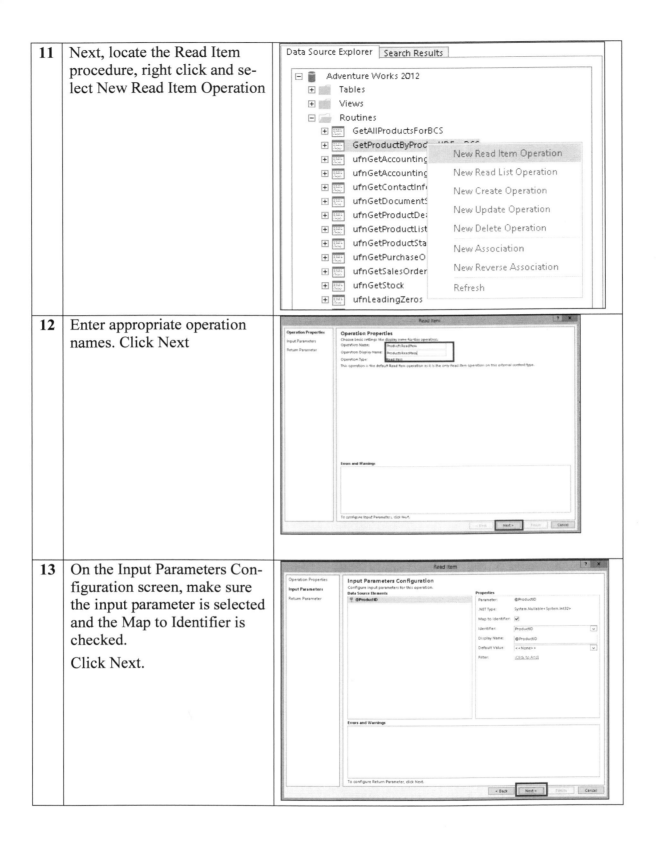
12	Enter appropriate operation names. Click Next	
13	On the Input Parameters Configuration screen, make sure the input parameter is selected and the Map to Identifier is checked. Click Next.	

| 14 | On the Return Parameter Configuration screen, make sure the row identifier (primary key) is selected and check the Map to Identifier checkbox. The Identifier, Field, and DisplayName become populated with the row identifier.

Click Finish. | 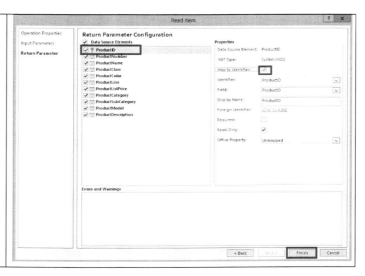 |

The new operations appear in the External Content Type Operations section

15	**Save the External Content Type**	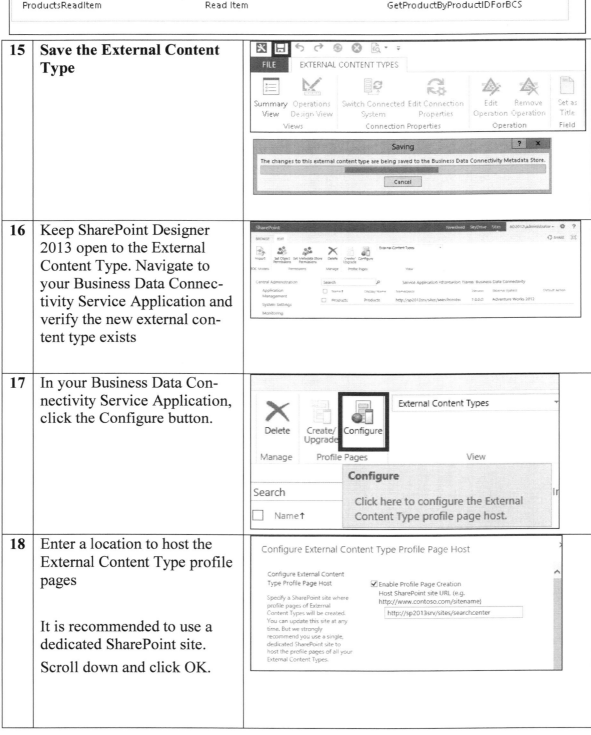
16	Keep SharePoint Designer 2013 open to the External Content Type. Navigate to your Business Data Connectivity Service Application and verify the new external content type exists	
17	In your Business Data Connectivity Service Application, click the Configure button.	
18	Enter a location to host the External Content Type profile pages It is recommended to use a dedicated SharePoint site. Scroll down and click OK.	

| 19 | Navigate back to SharePoint Designer 2013 and with the External Content Type opened, click on the Create Profile Page button from the top-ribbon

The Profile Page is created. This page becomes used for the search results URL if a custom URL (page) is not used as part of the data source. |  |

Task 11-4: Set Permissions on the BCS Entity

1	Navigate to your Business Data Connectivity Service Application and select the External Content Type by checking the checkbox Click on the Set Object Permissions button from the top-ribbon.	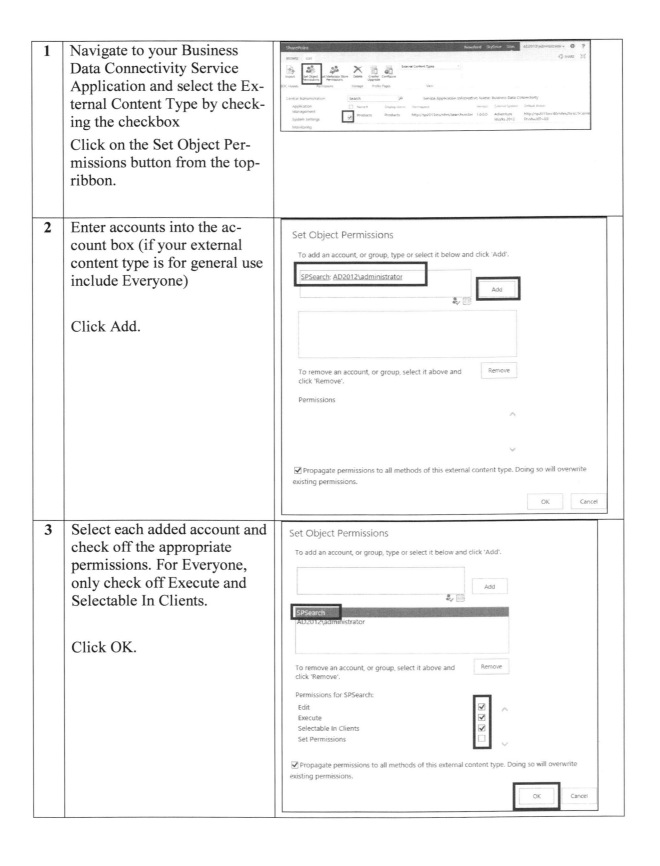
2	Enter accounts into the account box (if your external content type is for general use include Everyone) Click Add.	
3	Select each added account and check off the appropriate permissions. For Everyone, only check off Execute and Selectable In Clients. Click OK.	

Task 11-5: Create a Content Source for the External Content Type

1	Navigate to Central Administration and click on Manage service applications	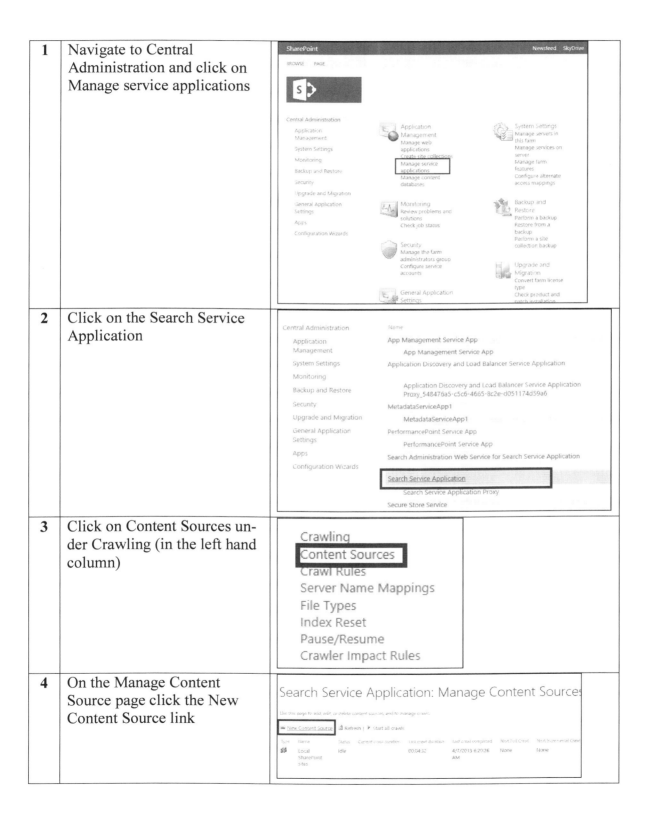
2	Click on the Search Service Application	
3	Click on Content Sources under Crawling (in the left hand column)	
4	On the Manage Content Source page click the New Content Source link	

5	Enter a name for the Content Source and select Line of Business Data. Select the Crawl selected external data source and check off the data source	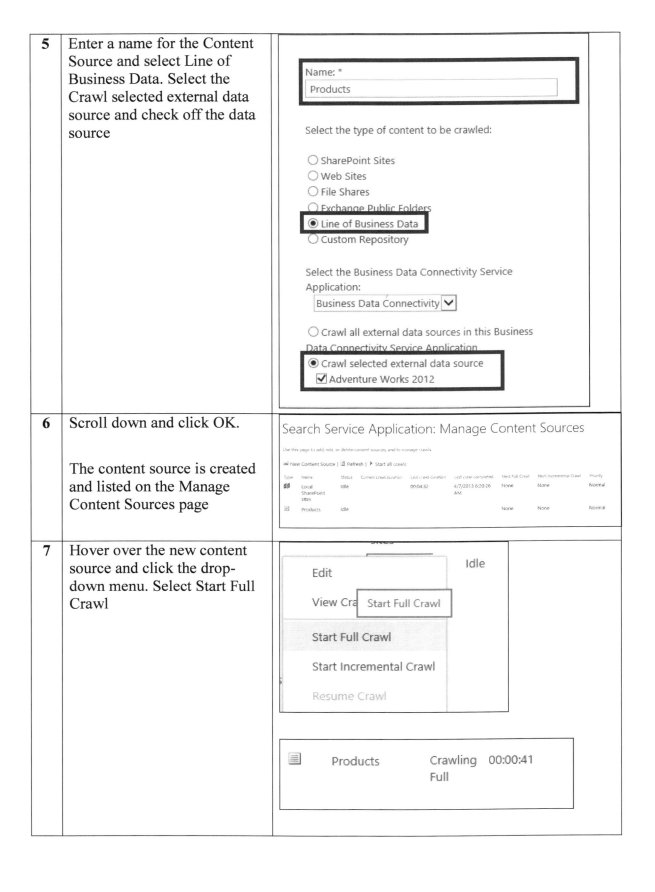
6	Scroll down and click OK. The content source is created and listed on the Manage Content Sources page	Search Service Application: Manage Content Sources Use this page to add, edit, or delete content sources, and to manage crawls. New Content Source | Refresh | ▶ Start all crawls Type Name Status Current crawl duration Last crawl duration Last crawl completed Need Full Crawl Next Incremental Crawl Priority Local SharePoint sites — Idle — 00:04:32 4/7/2013 6:20:26 AM None None Normal Products — Idle — — — None None Normal
7	Hover over the new content source and click the drop-down menu. Select Start Full Crawl	SITES Idle Edit View Cra [Start Full Crawl] Start Full Crawl Start Incremental Crawl Resume Crawl Products Crawling 00:00:41 Full

Task 11-6: Create Managed Properties Based on Crawled Properties

After the crawl has completed, you now need to create managed properties and map them to the crawled properties from the new content source. This may be accomplished from the Search Service Application UI or from PowerShell. Either way, you need to know what crawled properties have been created.

1	From the Search Service Application, click on Search Schema on the left hand side of the screen under Queries and Results	Queries and Results Authoritative Pages Result Sources Query Rules Query Client Types Search Schema Query Suggestions Search Dictionaries Search Result Removal
2	On the Managed Properties page, click on Crawled Properties at the top	Search Service Application: Managed Properties Managed Properties | Crawled Properties | Categories Use this page to view, create, or modify managed properties and map crawled properties to managed properties. Crawled properties are auto... properties will take effect after the next full crawl. Note that the settings that you can adjust depend on your current authorization level.

3	Select Business Data from the Category drop-down and click the filter button
	
	The crawled properties from the external data source are displayed
		Filters
		
		Crawled properties
		Category Business Data
		     ☐ Show unaltered property names
		     ➡

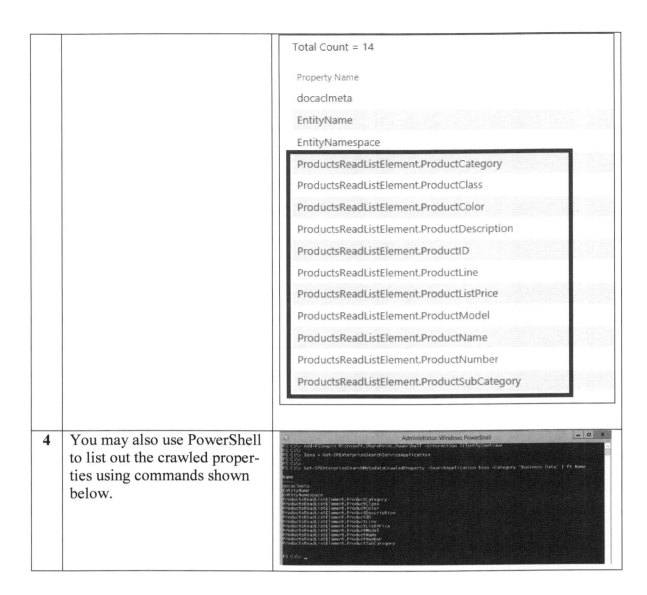

| 4 | You may also use PowerShell to list out the crawled properties using commands shown below. | |

Add-PSSnapin Microsoft.SharePoint.PowerShell -ErrorAction SilentlyContinue

$ssa = Get-SPEnterpriseSearchServiceApplication

Get-SPEnterpriseSearchMetadataCrawledProperty -SearchApplication $ssa -Category 'Business Data' | ft Name

Now that you know what the crawled properties are, you can map them to managed properties. If the managed properties were already created, you could simply click on each crawled property on the Crawled Property page and map them. In this case, there are no managed properties yet.

| 5 | Click on the Managed Properties link at the top of the Crawled Properties page | Search Service Application: Crawled Properties

Managed Properties Crawled Properties \| Categories |

6	On the Managed Properties page, click on New Managed Property	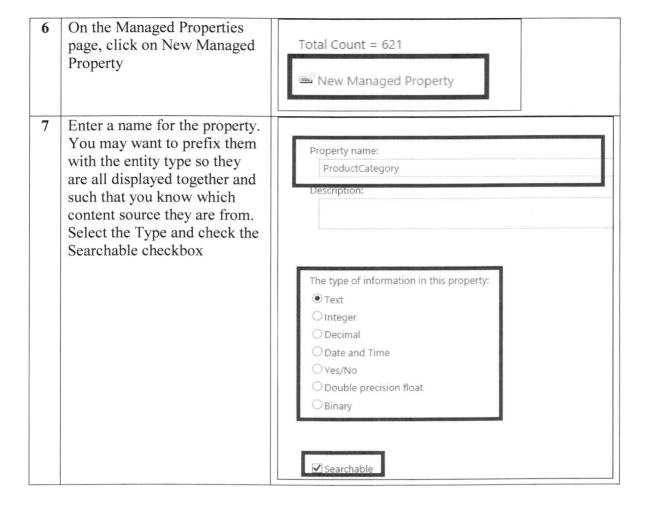
7	Enter a name for the property. You may want to prefix them with the entity type so they are all displayed together and such that you know which content source they are from. Select the Type and check the Searchable checkbox	

8	Scroll down and check Queryable and Retrievable. For this example, the Product Category will be refinable and sortable so select "Yes - active" for both of these entries

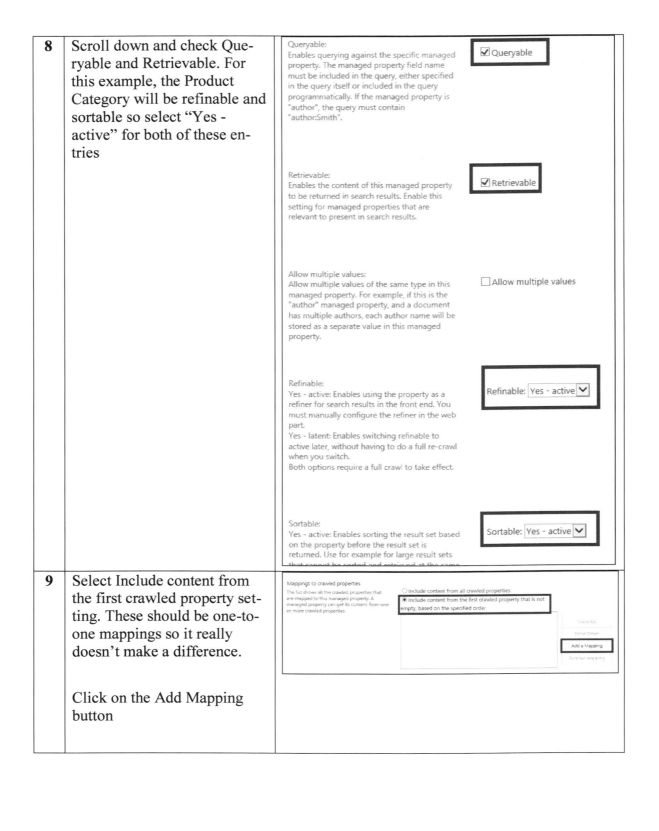

Queryable:
Enables querying against the specific managed property. The managed property field name must be included in the query, either specified in the query itself or included in the query programmatically. If the managed property is "author", the query must contain "author:Smith".

☑ Queryable

Retrievable:
Enables the content of this managed property to be returned in search results. Enable this setting for managed properties that are relevant to present in search results.

☑ Retrievable

Allow multiple values:
Allow multiple values of the same type in this managed property. For example, if this is the "author" managed property, and a document has multiple authors, each author name will be stored as a separate value in this managed property.

☐ Allow multiple values

Refinable:
Yes - active: Enables using the property as a refiner for search results in the front end. You must manually configure the refiner in the web part.
Yes - latent: Enables switching refinable to active later, without having to do a full re-crawl when you switch.
Both options require a full crawl to take effect.

Refinable: Yes - active ▼

Sortable:
Yes - active: Enables sorting the result set based on the property before the result set is returned. Use for example for large result sets

Sortable: Yes - active ▼

| 9 | Select Include content from the first crawled property setting. These should be one-to-one mappings so it really doesn't make a difference.

Click on the Add Mapping button |
|---|---|

Mappings to crawled properties
The list shows all the crawled properties that are mapped to this managed property. A managed property can get its content from one or more crawled properties.

○ Include content from all crawled properties
● Include content from the first crawled property that is not empty, based on the specified order

Add a Mapping

10	In the Crawled property dialog, select Business Data from the filter drop-down. Select the appropriate crawled property and click OK.	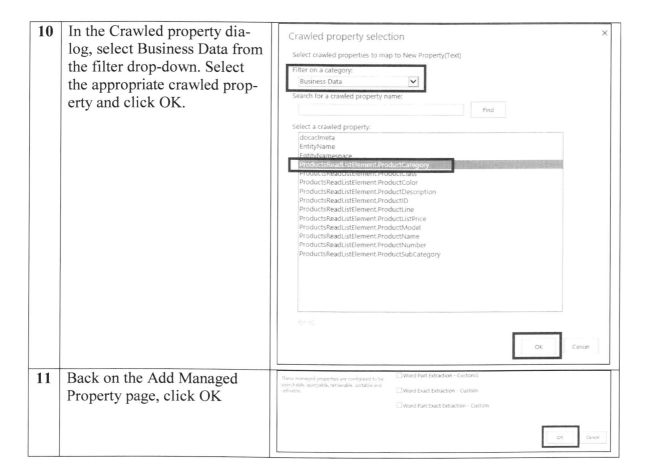
11	Back on the Add Managed Property page, click OK	

You'll need to repeat this process for each crawled property.

Performing the mapping through the UI can become tedious. That's why it may be easier to create a script to map all of your properties via PowerShell:

Add-PSSnapin Microsoft.SharePoint.PowerShell -ErrorAction SilentlyContinue

$ssa = Get-SPEnterpriseSearchServiceApplication

$crawledProperty = Get-SPEnterpriseSearchMetadataCrawledProperty -SearchApplication $ssa -Name ProductsReadListElement.ProductCategory

$managedProperty = New-SPEnterpriseSearchMetadataManagedProperty -SearchApplication $ssa -Name ProductCategory -FullTextQueriable$true -Queryable$true -Retrievable$true -Type 1

New-SPEnterpriseSearchMetadataMapping -SearchApplication $ssa -ManagedProperty $managedProperty -CrawledProperty $crawledProperty

Simply repeat the last three lines for each property mapping.

There are no parameters for sortable or refinable so use the UI and change those settings manually for the properties you want to sort or refine. You could create the crawled property if you knew what it was going to be named but in the example script the crawled property is retrieved since it was already created.

```
Administrator: Windows PowerShell                    _ □ X

PS C:\> .\cp.ps1

CrawledPropset           : 2edeba9a-0fa8-4020-8a8b-30c3cdf34ccd
CrawledPropertyName      : ProductsReadListElement.ProductCategory
CrawledPropertyVariantType : 0
ManagedPid               : 1016

CrawledPropset           : 2edeba9a-0fa8-4020-8a8b-30c3cdf34ccd
CrawledPropertyName      : ProductsReadListElement.ProductClass
CrawledPropertyVariantType : 0
ManagedPid               : 1017

CrawledPropset           : 2edeba9a-0fa8-4020-8a8b-30c3cdf34ccd
CrawledPropertyName      : ProductsReadListElement.ProductColor
CrawledPropertyVariantType : 0
ManagedPid               : 1018

CrawledPropset           : 2edeba9a-0fa8-4020-8a8b-30c3cdf34ccd
CrawledPropertyName      : ProductsReadListElement.ProductDescription
CrawledPropertyVariantType : 0
ManagedPid               : 1019

CrawledPropset           : 2edeba9a-0fa8-4020-8a8b-30c3cdf34ccd
CrawledPropertyName      : ProductsReadListElement.ProductID
CrawledPropertyVariantType : 0
ManagedPid               : 1020

CrawledPropset           : 2edeba9a-0fa8-4020-8a8b-30c3cdf34ccd
CrawledPropertyName      : ProductsReadListElement.ProductLine
CrawledPropertyVariantType : 0
ManagedPid               : 1021

CrawledPropset           : 2edeba9a-0fa8-4020-8a8b-30c3cdf34ccd
CrawledPropertyName      : ProductsReadListElement.ProductListPrice
CrawledPropertyVariantType : 0
ManagedPid               : 1022

CrawledPropset           : 2edeba9a-0fa8-4020-8a8b-30c3cdf34ccd
CrawledPropertyName      : ProductsReadListElement.ProductModel
CrawledPropertyVariantType : 0
ManagedPid               : 1023

CrawledPropset           : 2edeba9a-0fa8-4020-8a8b-30c3cdf34ccd
CrawledPropertyName      : ProductsReadListElement.ProductName
CrawledPropertyVariantType : 0
ManagedPid               : 1024

CrawledPropset           : 2edeba9a-0fa8-4020-8a8b-30c3cdf34ccd
CrawledPropertyName      : ProductsReadListElement.ProductNumber
CrawledPropertyVariantType : 0
ManagedPid               : 1025

CrawledPropset           : 2edeba9a-0fa8-4020-8a8b-30c3cdf34ccd
CrawledPropertyName      : ProductsReadListElement.ProductSubCategory
CrawledPropertyVariantType : 0
ManagedPid               : 1026
```

In order for the Managed Properties to take effect, you now need to run a full crawl on the content source again.

Task 11-7: Create a Result Source for the New Content Source

1	Navigate to your Search Center and select Site Settings from the Settings menu	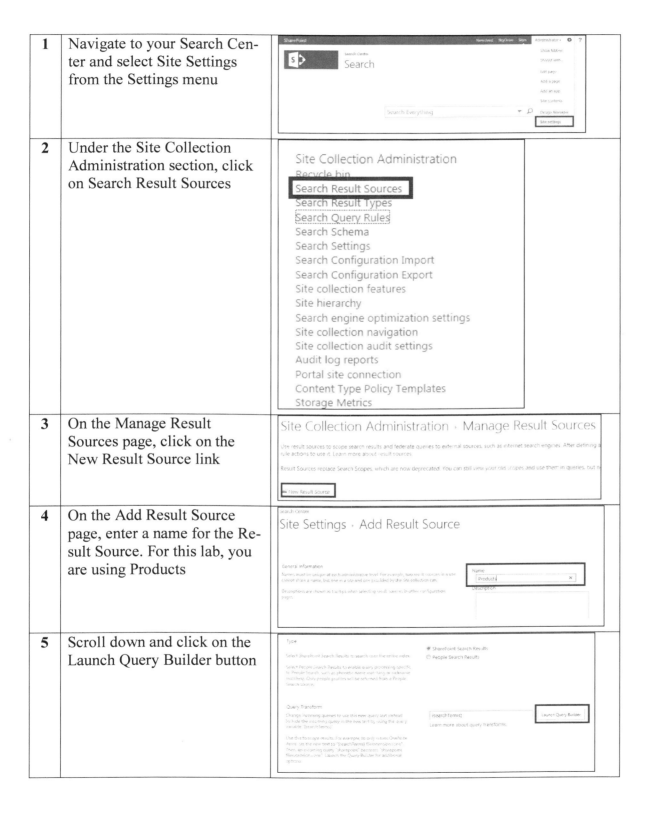
2	Under the Site Collection Administration section, click on Search Result Sources	
3	On the Manage Result Sources page, click on the New Result Source link	
4	On the Add Result Source page, enter a name for the Result Source. For this lab, you are using Products	
5	Scroll down and click on the Launch Query Builder button	

6	In the Property Filter section, first select "--Show all managed properties--"	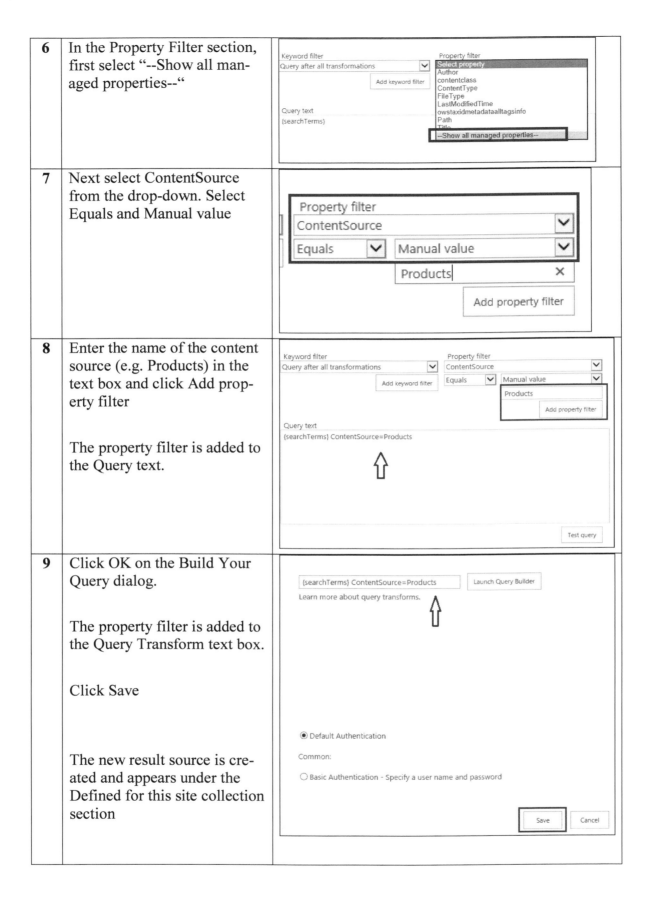
7	Next select ContentSource from the drop-down. Select Equals and Manual value	
8	Enter the name of the content source (e.g. Products) in the text box and click Add property filter The property filter is added to the Query text.	
9	Click OK on the Build Your Query dialog. The property filter is added to the Query Transform text box. Click Save The new result source is created and appears under the Defined for this site collection section	

Search Center

Site Collection Administration

Use result sources to scope search results and federate queries to exter

Result Sources replace Search Scopes, which are now deprecated. You

New Result Source

Name

Defined for this site collection (1)

Products

Provided by SharePoint (16)

Task 11-8: Create a Result Type for the Result Source

1	Navigate to your Search Center and select Site Settings from the Settings menu. Under the Site Collection Administration section, click on the Search Result Types link	Site Collection Administration Recycle bin Search Result Sources **Search Result Types** Search Query Rules Search Schema Search Settings Search Configuration Import Search Configuration Export Site collection features Site hierarchy Search engine optimization settings Site collection navigation
2	On the Result Types page click on the New Result Type link	Search Center **S** **Site Collection Administration** Tailor the look of important result types by crafting a display template in HTML and defining a rule tha priority. Learn more about how to configure result types. New Result Type
3	Enter a name for the Result Type. Select the Result Source created in the previous task section from the source drop-down. Skip the types of content rule. Select Default Item for now under "What should these results look like?". You will create a custom item template in later tasks. Click Save.	Search Center **Site Collection Administration › Add Result Type** apply to all sites in the site collection. To make one for just this site, use site result types. Give it a name [Products] Which source should results match? [Products ▼] What types of content should match? You can skip this rule to match all content [Select a value ▼] Add value What should these results look like? [Default Item ▼] Note: This result type will automatically update with the latest properties in your display template each time you visit the Manage Result Types Page. Display template URL [~sitecollection~ catalogs/masterpage/Display Templates/Search/Item_Default.js] ☐ Optimize for frequent use [Save] [Cancel]

Task 11-9: Create a Search Results Page for the New Content Source

1	Navigate to your Search Center and select Site Contents from the Settings menu	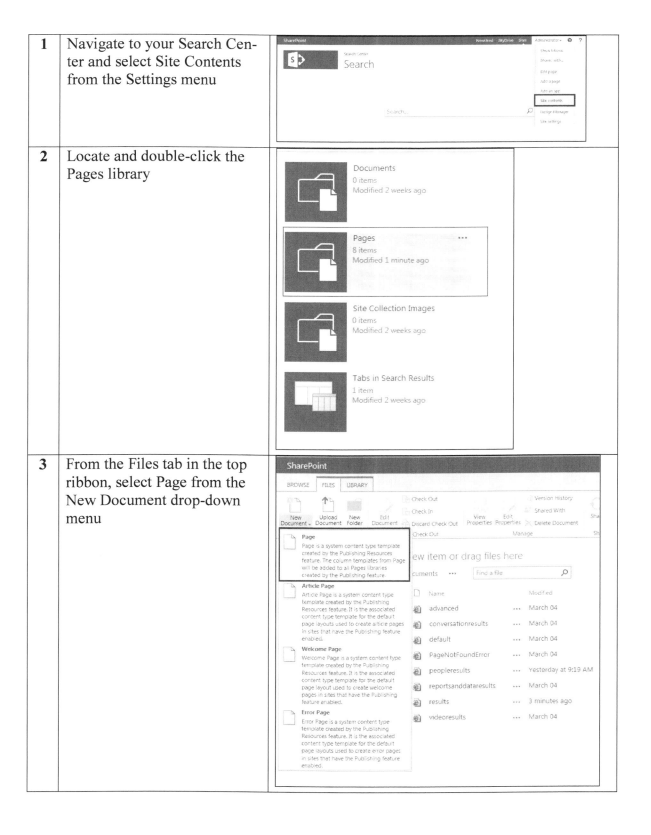
2	Locate and double-click the Pages library	
3	From the Files tab in the top ribbon, select Page from the New Document drop-down menu	

4	On the Create Page page, enter a title and URL Name. Click Create.	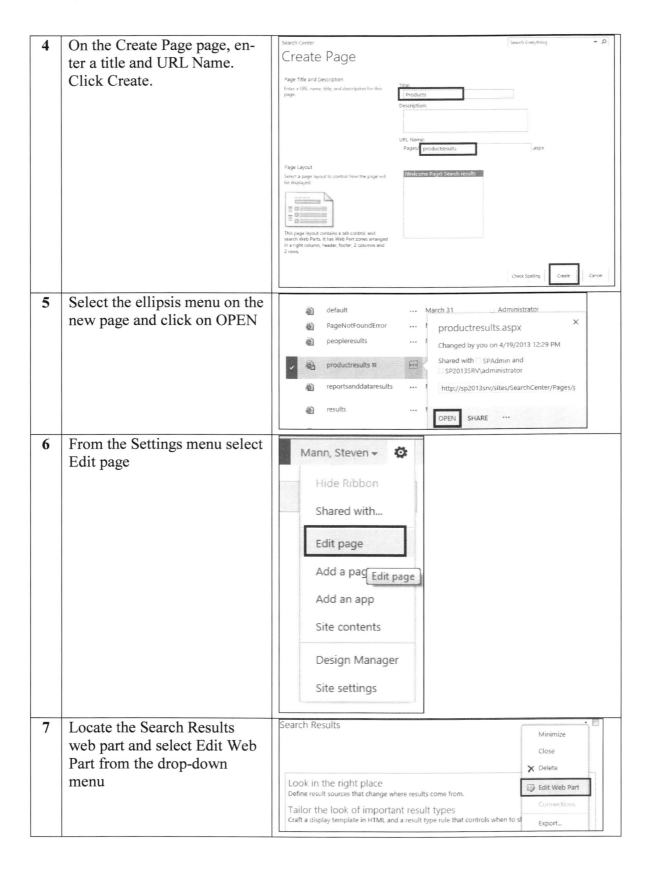
5	Select the ellipsis menu on the new page and click on OPEN	
6	From the Settings menu select Edit page	
7	Locate the Search Results web part and select Edit Web Part from the drop-down menu	

8	In the Properties tool pane that appeared on the right, click the Change query button. The Build Your Query dialog appears.	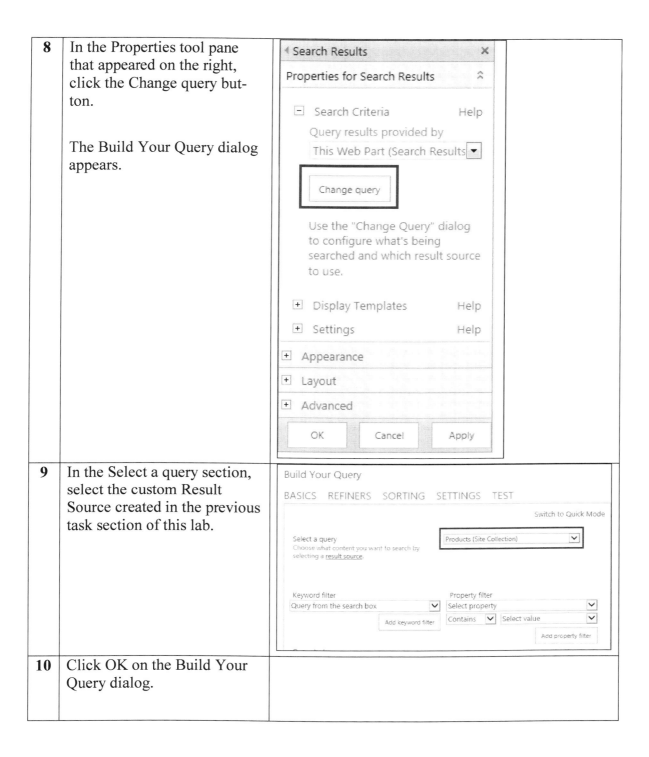
9	In the Select a query section, select the custom Result Source created in the previous task section of this lab.	
10	Click OK on the Build Your Query dialog.	

11	Click OK in the web part properties tool pane	Search Results ◄ ✕ Properties for Search Results ⌃ ⊟ Search Criteria Help Query results provided by This Web Part (Search Results ▾) Change query Use the "Change Query" dialog to configure what's being searched and which result source to use. ⊞ Display Templates Help ⊞ Settings Help ⊞ Appearance ⊞ Layout ⊞ Advanced OK Cancel Apply	
12	Check in the page		
13	Publish the page		

Task 11-10: Add a Custom Results Page to the Search Center Navigation

1	Navigate to your Search Center and select Site Settings from the Settings menu	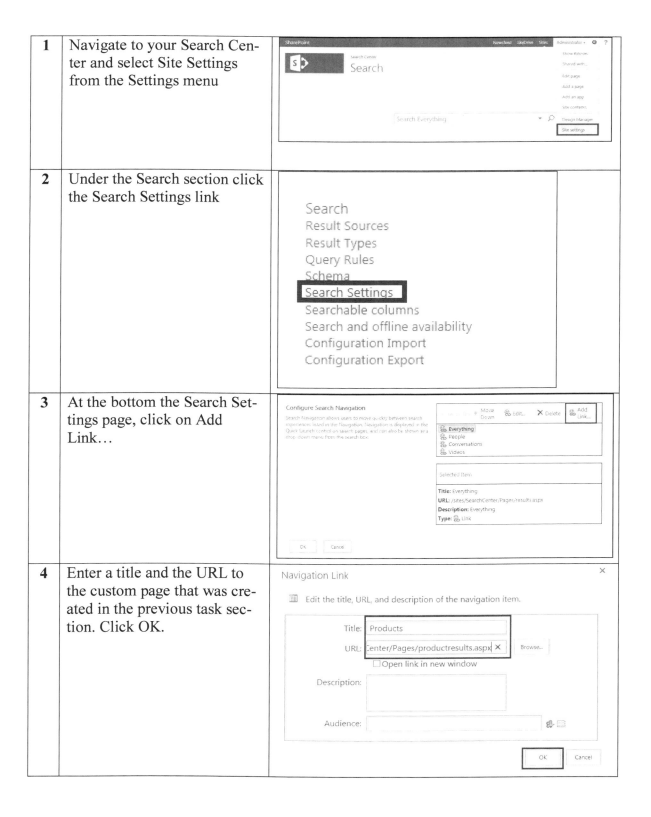
2	Under the Search section click the Search Settings link	
3	At the bottom the Search Settings page, click on Add Link…	
4	Enter a title and the URL to the custom page that was created in the previous task section. Click OK.	

| 5 | Back on the Search Settings page click OK | 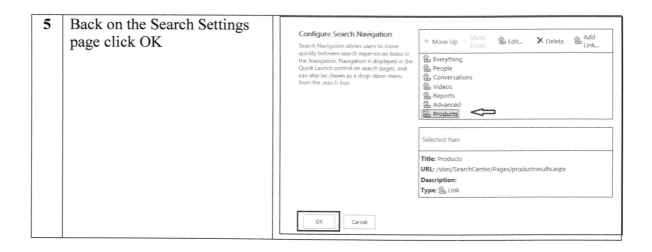 |

Task 11-11: Test the Results

1	Navigate to your Search Center. The new navigation item appears at the top. Click on the new link and perform a search	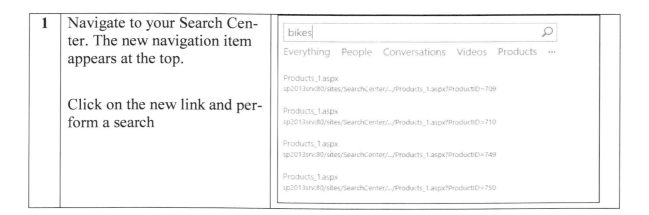

The results aren't too pretty. The next tasks explain how to create custom item templates and hover panels for the external content source.

Task 11-12: Create an Item Display Template

1	Fire up SharePoint Designer 2013 and Open the Search Center Site	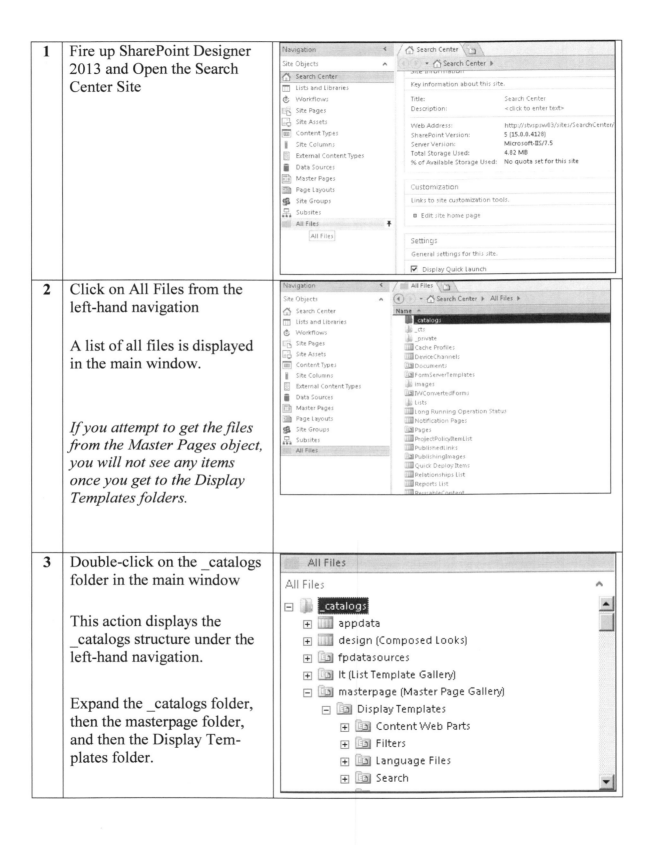
2	Click on All Files from the left-hand navigation A list of all files is displayed in the main window. *If you attempt to get the files from the Master Pages object, you will not see any items once you get to the Display Templates folders.*	
3	Double-click on the _catalogs folder in the main window This action displays the _catalogs structure under the left-hand navigation. Expand the _catalogs folder, then the masterpage folder, and then the Display Templates folder.	

4	Click on the Search folder under Display Templates The list of Search display templates is shown in the main window area.	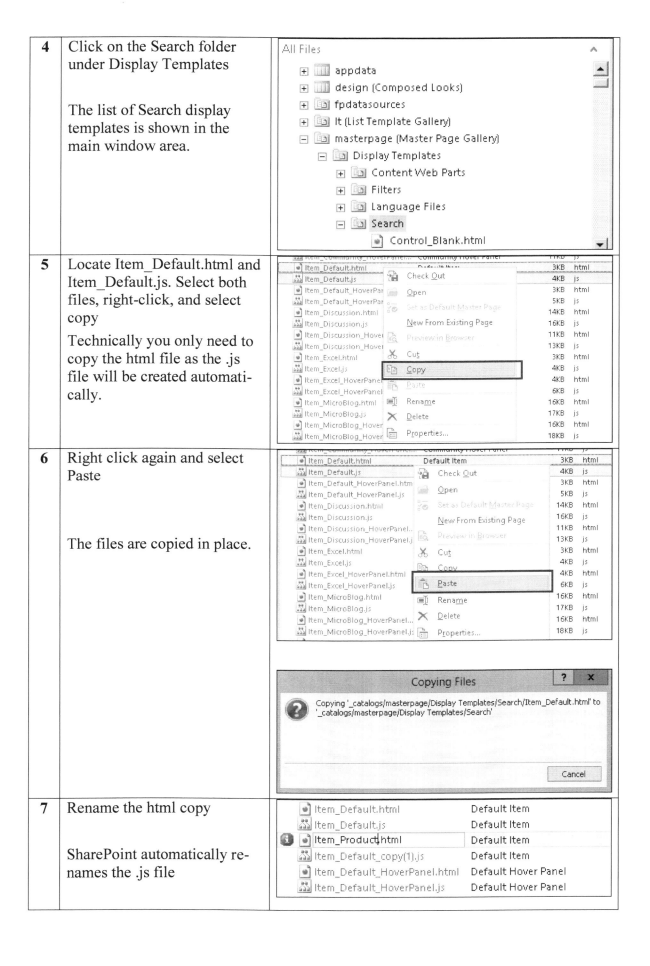
5	Locate Item_Default.html and Item_Default.js. Select both files, right-click, and select copy Technically you only need to copy the html file as the .js file will be created automatically.	
6	Right click again and select Paste The files are copied in place.	
7	Rename the html copy SharePoint automatically re-names the .js file	

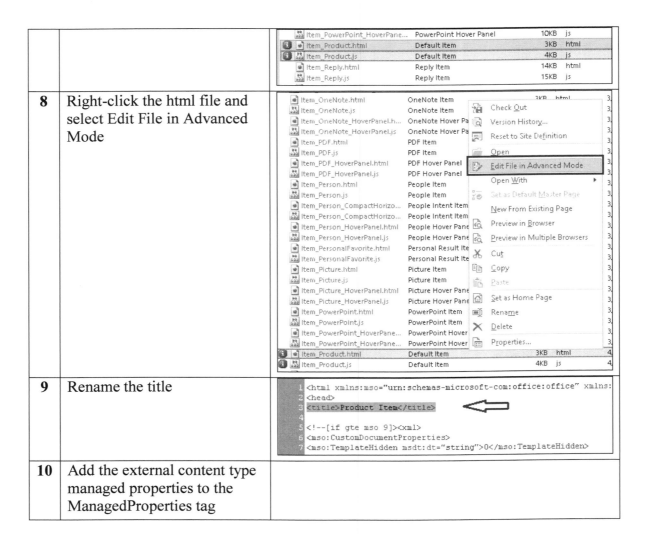

8	Right-click the html file and select Edit File in Advanced Mode	
9	Rename the title	
10	Add the external content type managed properties to the ManagedProperties tag	

Row 9 image shows:
```
1  <html xmlns:mso="urn:schemas-microsoft-com:office:office" xmlns:
2  <head>
3  <title>Product Item</title>
4
5  <!--[if gte mso 9]><xml>
6  <mso:CustomDocumentProperties>
7  <mso:TemplateHidden msdt:dt="string">0</mso:TemplateHidden>
```

'ProductSubCategory''ProductSubCategory','ProductNumber''ProductNumber',

(see code examples on www.SteveTheManMann.com)

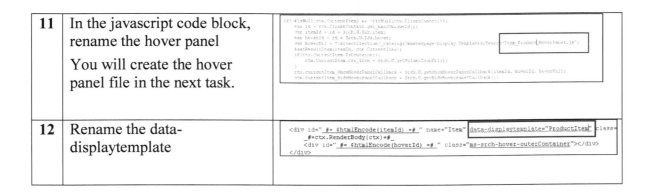

| 11 | In the javascript code block, rename the hover panel You will create the hover panel file in the next task. | |
| 12 | Rename the data-displaytemplate | |

13	In the javascript code block, create variables that determine if there is data in the managed property fields	

```
var has_name = !$isEmptyString(ctx.CurrentItem.ProductName);
var has_model = !$isEmptyString(ctx.CurrentItem.ProductModel);
var has_number = !$isEmptyString(ctx.CurrentItem.ProductNumber);
var has_category = !$isEmptyString(ctx.CurrentItem.ProductCategory);
```

14	Remove the ctx.RenderBody line	
15	For each managed property, create a code block similar to the following (see below) Save the html file.	

```
!--#
            if(has_number == true) {
  #-->
                <div id="ProductNumberField">
                <div id="ProductNumberValue" class="ms-srch-ellipsis" title="_#= ctx.CurrentItem.ProductNumber =#_">Product Number _#= ctx.CurrentItem.ProductNumber =#_ </div>
                </div>
<!--#
            }
  #-->
```

Code examples are available on www.SteveTheManMann.com.

Task 11-13: Create an Item Hover Panel

1	Back in the listing of display templates, locate and select the Item_Default_HoverPanel files. Right-click and select Copy	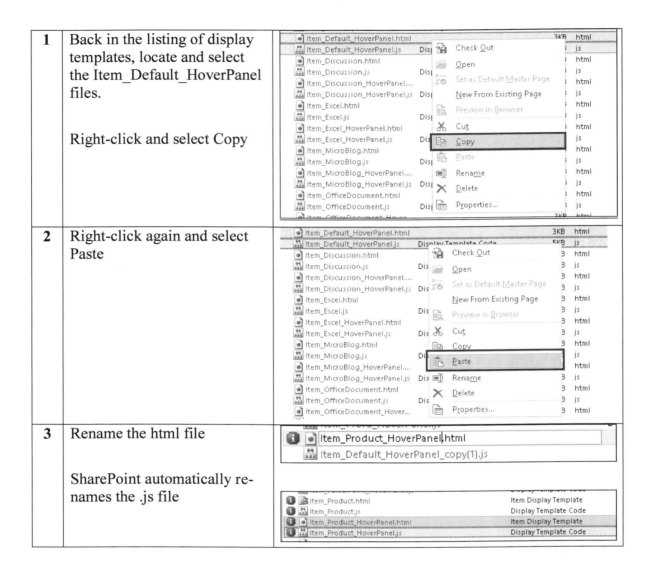
2	Right-click again and select Paste	
3	Rename the html file SharePoint automatically re-names the .js file	

4	Right click the html file and select Edit File in Advanced Mode	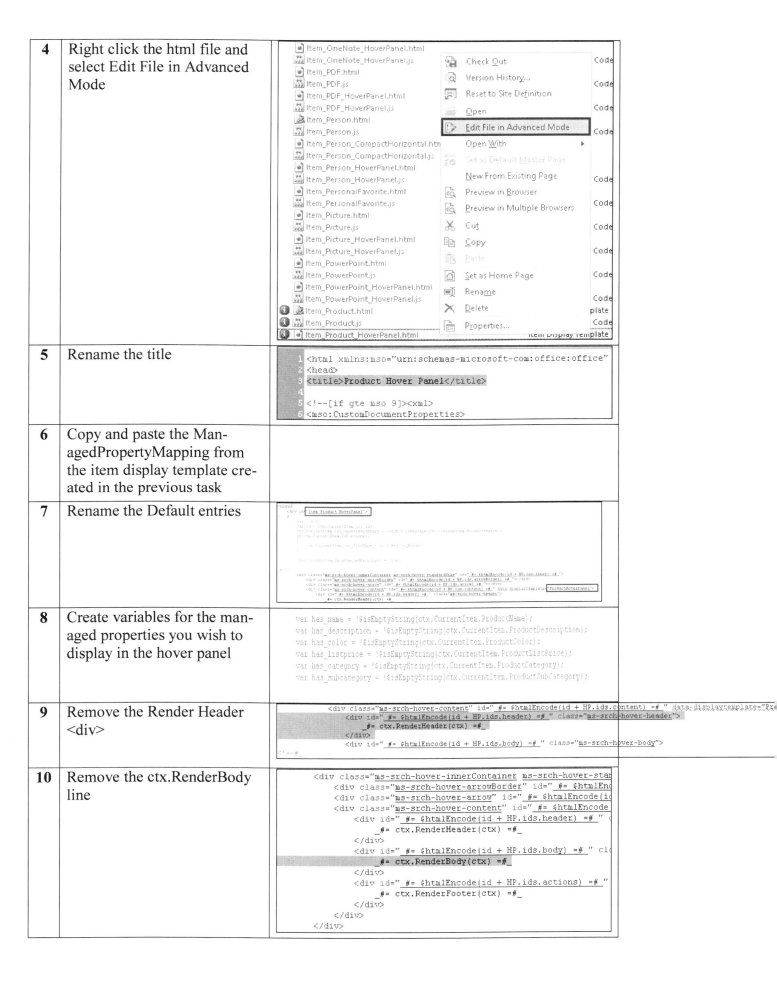
| 5 | Rename the title | ```
1  <html xmlns:mso="urn:schemas-microsoft-com:office:office"
2  <head>
3  <title>Product Hover Panel</title>
4
5  <!--[if gte mso 9]><xml>
6  <mso:CustomDocumentProperties>
``` |
| 6 | Copy and paste the ManagedPropertyMapping from the item display template created in the previous task | |
| 7 | Rename the Default entries | |
| 8 | Create variables for the managed properties you wish to display in the hover panel | ```
var has_name = !$isEmptyString(ctx.CurrentItem.ProductName);
var has_description = !$isEmptyString(ctx.CurrentItem.ProductDescription);
var has_color = !$isEmptyString(ctx.CurrentItem.ProductColor);
var has_listprice = !$isEmptyString(ctx.CurrentItem.ProductListPrice);
var has_category = !$isEmptyString(ctx.CurrentItem.ProductCategory);
var has_subcategory = !$isEmptyString(ctx.CurrentItem.ProductSubCategory);
``` |
| 9 | Remove the Render Header <div> | ```
<div class="ms-srch-hover-content" id="_#= $htmlEncode(id + HP.ids.content) =#_" data-displaytemplate="Pro
    <div id="_#= $htmlEncode(id + HP.ids.header) =#_" class="ms-srch-hover-header">
        _#= ctx.RenderHeader(ctx) =#_
    </div>
        <div id="_#= $htmlEncode(id + HP.ids.body) =#_" class="ms-srch-hover-body">
``` |
| 10 | Remove the ctx.RenderBody line | ```
<div class="ms-srch-hover-innerContainer ms-srch-hover-star
    <div class="ms-srch-hover-arrowBorder" id="_#= $htmlEnc
    <div class="ms-srch-hover-arrow" id="_#= $htmlEncode(id
    <div class="ms-srch-hover-content" id="_#= $htmlEncode
        <div id="_#= $htmlEncode(id + HP.ids.header) =#_" (
            _#= ctx.RenderHeader(ctx) =#_
        </div>
            <div id="_#= $htmlEncode(id + HP.ids.body) =#_" cla
                _#= ctx.RenderBody(ctx) =#_
            </div>
            <div id="_#= $htmlEncode(id + HP.ids.actions) =#_"
                _#= ctx.RenderFooter(ctx) =#_
            </div>
        </div>
    </div>
``` |

| 11 | Again, add code blocks for each managed property.

Example files are located on SteveTheManMann.com | ```html
<div id="_#= $htmlEncode(id + HP.ids.body) =#_" class="ms-srch-hover-body">

    if(has_name == true) {

        <div id="ProductNameField">
            <div id="ProductNameValue" class="ms-srch-ellipsis" style="font-weight:bold">
        </div>

    }

    if(has_description == true) {

        <div id="ProductDescriptionField">
            <div id="ProductDescriptionValue" class="ms-srch-ellipsis" title="_#= ctx.Cur
        </div>

    }

    if(has_color == true) {

        <div id="ProductColorField">
            <div id="ProductColorValue" class="ms-srch-ellipsis" title="_#= ctx.CurrentI
        </div>

    }
``` |
| 12 | Save the file. | |

```html
<div id="_#= $htmlEncode(id + HP.ids.body) =#_" class="ms-srch-hover-body">

    if(has_name == true) {

        <div id="ProductNameField">
            <div id="ProductNameValue" class="ms-srch-ellipsis" style="font-weight:bold"
```

Task 11-14: Update the Result Type to Use the New Display Template

1	Navigate to your Search Center and select Site Settings from the Settings menu. Under the Site Collection Administration section, click on the Search Result Types link	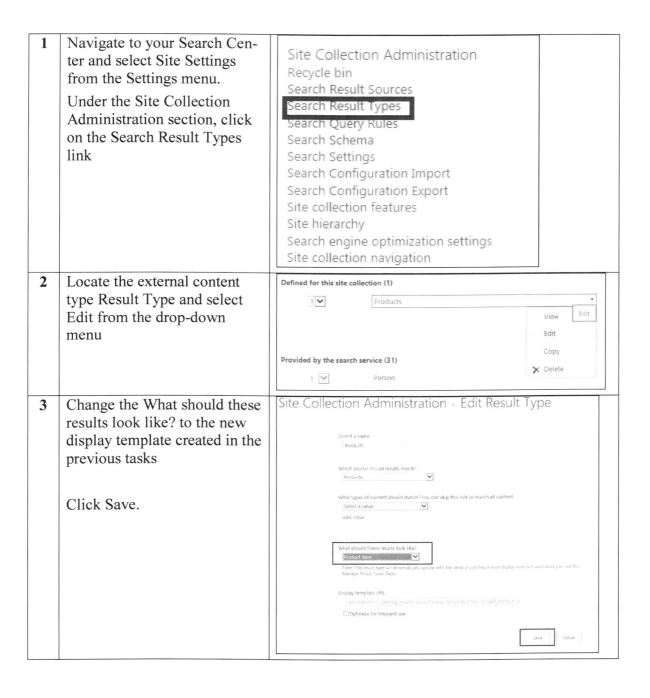
2	Locate the external content type Result Type and select Edit from the drop-down menu	
3	Change the What should these results look like? to the new display template created in the previous tasks Click Save.	

Task 11-15: Test the Item Display Template and Hover Panel

| 1 | Navigate to your Search Center and perform a search within the new results page

The results are shown with the managed property values and the hover panel displays additional information. | Product Number: SO-B909-M
Product Name: Mountain Bike Socks, M
Product Model: Mountain Bike Socks
Product Category: Clothing

Product Number: SO-B909-L
Product Name: Mountain Bike Socks, L
Product Model: Mountain Bike Socks
Product Category: Clothing

Product Number: BK-R93R-62
Product Name: Road-150 Red, 62
Product Model: Road-150
Product Category: Bikes

Product Number: BK-R93R-44
Product Name: Road-150 Red, 44
Product Model: Road-150
Product Category: Bikes

Product Number: BK-R93R-48
Product Name: Road-150 Red, 48
Product Model: Road-150
Product Category: Bikes | **Road-150 Red, 62**
This bike is ridden by race winners. Developed with the Adventure Works Cycles professional race team, it has a extremely light heat-treated aluminum frame, and steering that allows precision control.

Color: Red
List Price: 3578.27
Product Category: Bikes
Product SubCategory: Road Bikes

OPEN   SEND |

Task 11-16: Add Custom Sort Options

Now that you have results from your external content type, it would be nice if the user could sort their search results based on some of the managed properties that are now available. Properties used for sorting must be configured as Sortable.

1	Navigate to the custom results page that was created for the external content type and use the Settings menu to edit the page	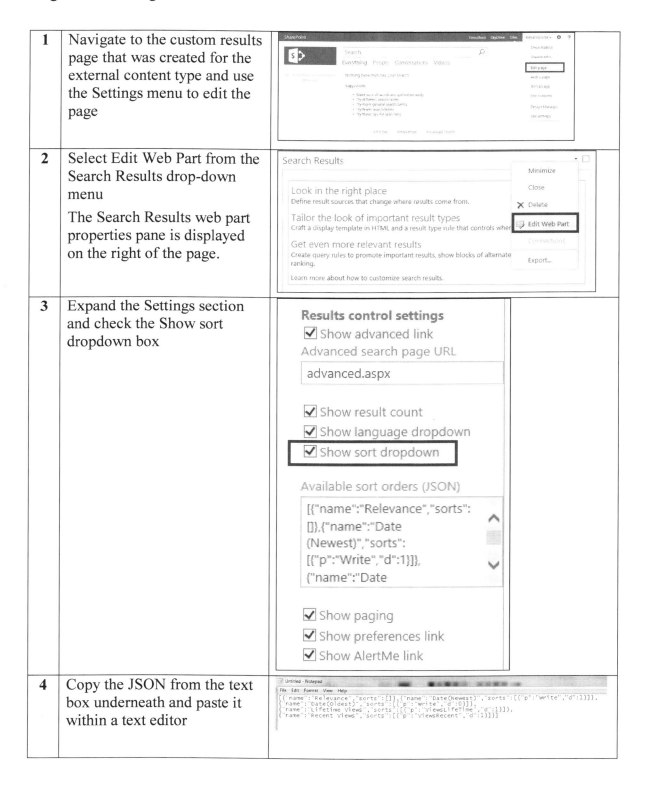
2	Select Edit Web Part from the Search Results drop-down menu The Search Results web part properties pane is displayed on the right of the page.	
3	Expand the Settings section and check the Show sort dropdown box	
4	Copy the JSON from the text box underneath and paste it within a text editor	

		Line breaks were entered for presentation purposes.
5	For this example, remove the Date sorts and replace them with Category and Color	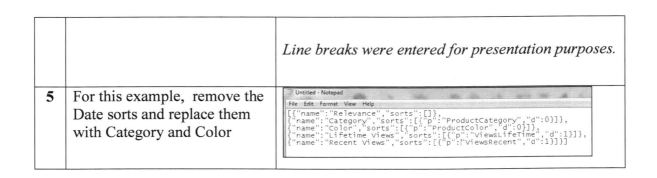

[{"name"""Relevance","sorts"[]},

{"name"""Category","sorts"[{"p"""ProductCategory","d"0}]},

{"name"""Color","sorts"[{"p"""ProductColor","d"0}]},

{"name"""Lifetime Views","sorts"[{"p"""ViewsLifeTime","d"1}]},

{"name"""Recent Views","sorts"[{"p"""ViewsRecent","d"1}]}]

6	Copy and Paste the modifications back into the text box within the web part properties. Click OK on the web part properties pane.	
7	**Check in the page** ⚠ **Checked out to you** Only you can see your recent changes. Check it in. ⟸ **Publish the page** ⚠ **Recent draft not published** Visitors can't see recent changes. Publish this draft. ⟸	

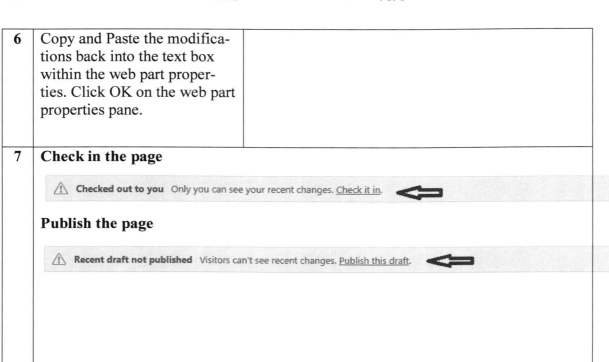

The Search Results page now displays a sort drop-down at the top of the page

Selecting a sort option displays the search results sorted by the selected property

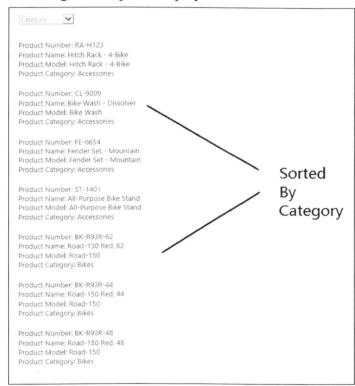

Task 11-17: Add Custom Refinements

You may also use the managed properties to provide the user options in refining the search results. Properties used for refinement must be configured as Refinable.

1	Navigate to the custom results page that was created for the external content type and use the Settings menu to edit the page	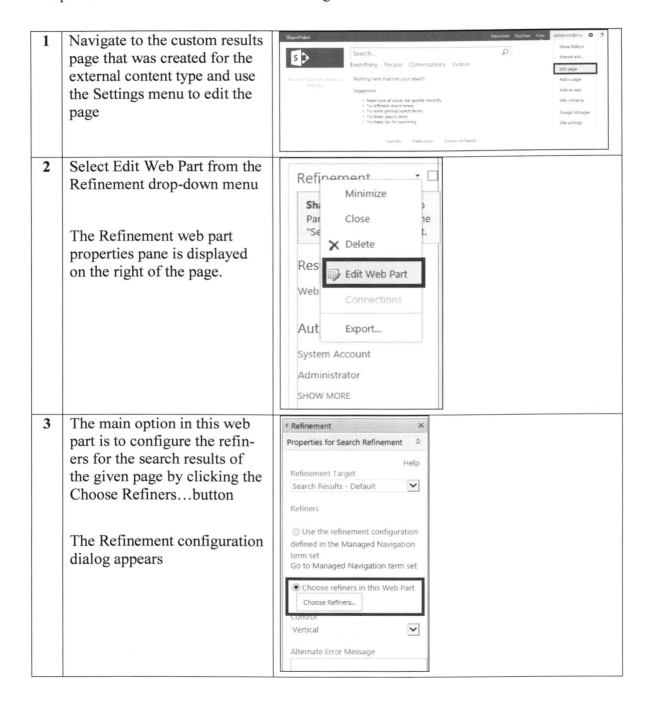
2	Select Edit Web Part from the Refinement drop-down menu The Refinement web part properties pane is displayed on the right of the page.	
3	The main option in this web part is to configure the refiners for the search results of the given page by clicking the Choose Refiners...button The Refinement configuration dialog appears	

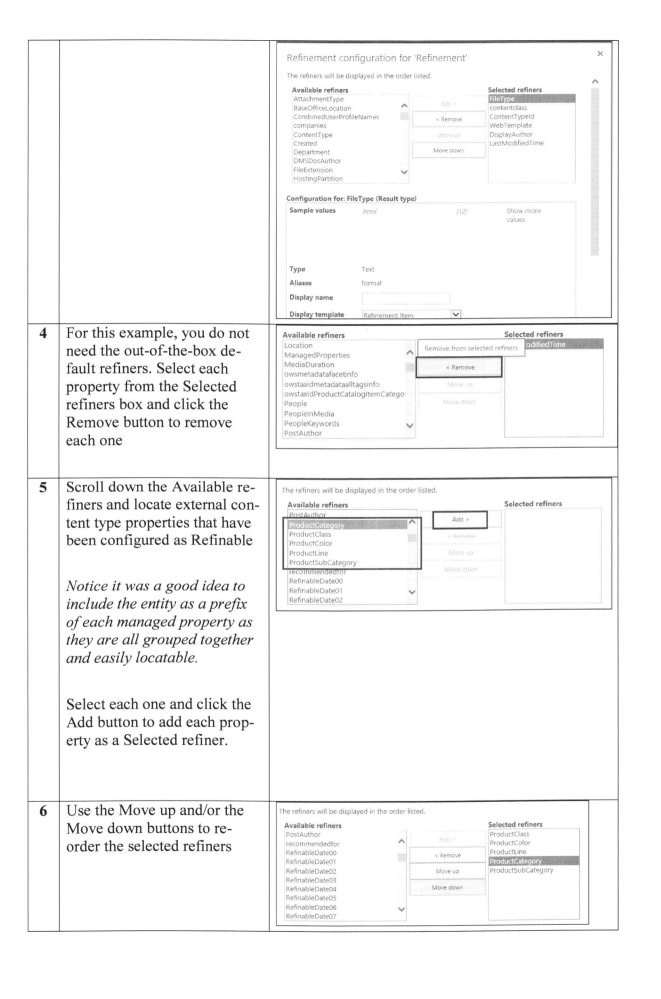

4	For this example, you do not need the out-of-the-box default refiners. Select each property from the Selected refiners box and click the Remove button to remove each one	
5	Scroll down the Available refiners and locate external content type properties that have been configured as Refinable *Notice it was a good idea to include the entity as a prefix of each managed property as they are all grouped together and easily locatable.* Select each one and click the Add button to add each property as a Selected refiner.	
6	Use the Move up and/or the Move down buttons to re-order the selected refiners	

7	Select each property and enter a Display name, Sort by, and Sort direction	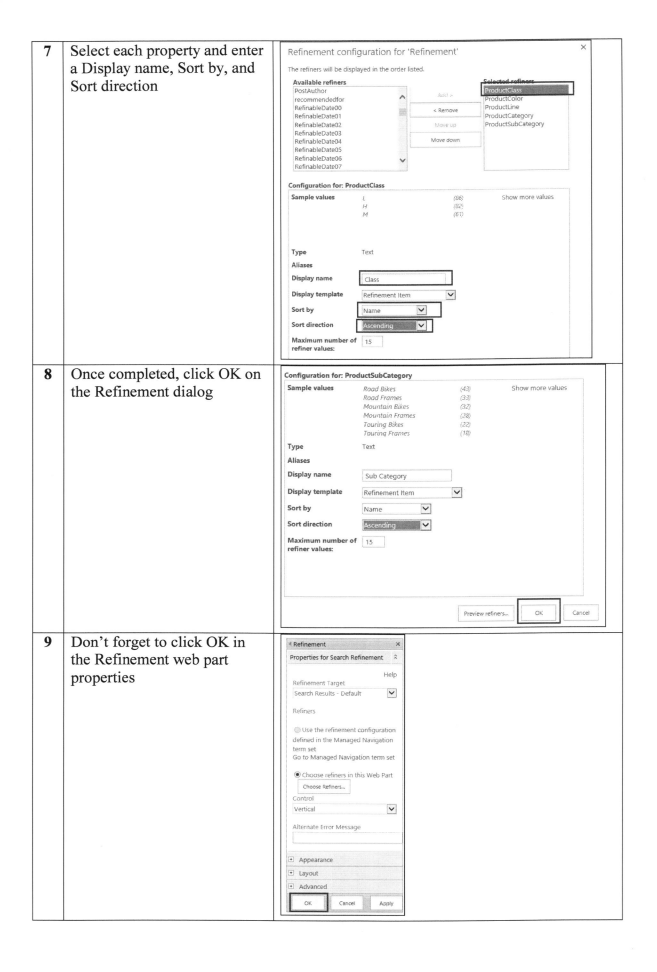
8	Once completed, click OK on the Refinement dialog	
9	Don't forget to click OK in the Refinement web part properties	

10	**Check in the page**
	⚠ **Checked out to you** Only you can see your recent changes. Check it in. ⬅
	Publish the page
	⚠ **Recent draft not published** Visitors can't see recent changes. Publish this draft. ⬅
11	Perform a search. The custom refinements appear on the left-hand side of the results page 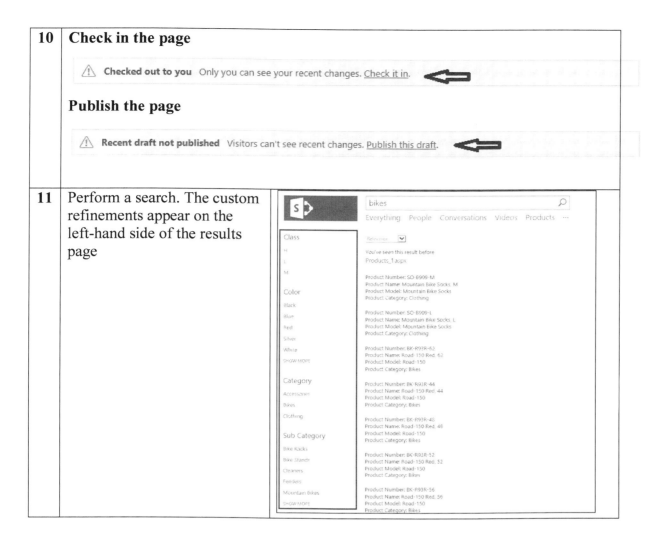

Suggestions

This lab explains suggestions and shows you how to add your own list of suggestions to SharePoint search.

Suggestions Overview

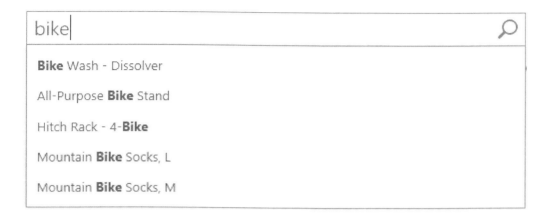

Suggestions are words or phrases that appear automatically when a user is typing search terms into a search box. Suggestions are enabled by default in both the Search Service Application and the Search Box web parts.

SharePoint automatically adds terms to the internal suggestion list based on user search actions. Once a term has been searched/queried and a result clicked a total of six (6) times, that term becomes part of the suggestion list.

This allows the suggestions to grow organically within your organization based on user past user search experiences. However, you may also add a list of suggestions to SharePoint to use. The tasks to follow show you how to do just that.

When you add a list of suggestions to the Search Service Application, all previous suggestions are removed. Therefore, it is a good idea to start off with a suggestion list before going live with your new Search Center.

Task 12-1: Create a Suggestion File

A suggestion file is just a text file that contains a word or phrase on each line. It may be anything that you feel will help your user search content. Some ideas include listing out products, clients/customers, contacts, etc. and using those values in the suggestion text file.

| 1 | For example purposes, list out all of the product names from the previous labs. | 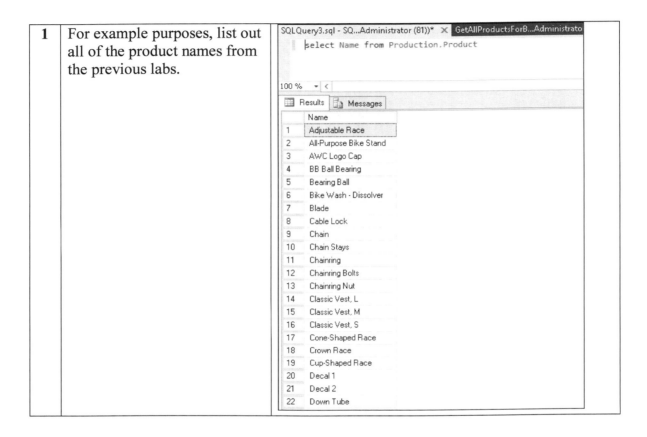 |

| 2 | Copy and paste the list into a text file | Suggestions.txt - Notepad

File Edit Format View Help

Adjustable Race
All-Purpose Bike Stand
AWC Logo Cap
BB Ball Bearing
Bearing Ball
Bike Wash - Dissolver
Blade
Cable Lock
Chain
Chain Stays
Chainring
Chainring Bolts
Chainring Nut
Classic Vest, L
Classic Vest, M
Classic Vest, S
Cone-Shaped Race
Crown Race
Cup-Shaped Race
Decal 1
Decal 2
Down Tube
External Lock Washer 1
External Lock Washer 2
External Lock Washer 3
External Lock Washer 4
External Lock Washer 5
External Lock Washer 6
External Lock Washer 7
External Lock Washer 8
External Lock Washer 9
Fender Set - Mountain
Flat Washer 1
Flat Washer 2
Flat Washer 3
Flat Washer 4
Flat Washer 5
Flat Washer 6
Flat Washer 7 |
| 3 | Save the text file and get ready for import. | |

Task 12-2: Import the Suggestion File

1	To import a suggestion file, navigate to your Search Service Application and click on Query Suggestions under the Queries and Results section of the left-hand navigation	Queries and Results Authoritative Pages Result Sources Query Rules Query Client Types Search Schema Query Suggestions Search Dictionaries Search Result Removal
2	Click on the Import from text file link on the Query Suggestion Settings page	Query Suggestion Settings Search Suggestions Show search suggestions as users type in the search box (if not disabled by user). ☑ Show search suggestions Language for suggestion phrases Choose the language for which to import and export query suggestion phrases. Language: English ▼ Always suggest phrases Always suggest the following list of phrases. Always suggest phrases: Import from text file Export to text file Never suggest phrases Never suggest the following list of phrases. Never suggest phrases: Import from text file Export to text file Save Settings Cancel
3	Click the Browse button to locate and select your suggestion text file Click OK.	Import phrases for query suggestions Use this page to import a text file containing a list of phrases for query suggestions. Text file with phrases The file is interpreted as one phrase per line. All existing phrases will be removed before importing phrases from the file. File with phrases to always suggest in English C:\QuerySuggestions_alwayssuggest.TXT Browse... OK Cancel
4	For good measure, click Save Settings	Query Suggestion Settings Search Suggestions Show search suggestions as users type in the search box (if not disabled by user). ☑ Show search suggestions Language for suggestion phrases Choose the language for which to import and export query suggestion phrases. Language: English ▼ Always suggest phrases Always suggest the following list of phrases. Always suggest phrases: Import from text file Export to text file Never suggest phrases Never suggest the following list of phrases. Never suggest phrases: Import from text file Export to text file Save Settings Cancel

Task 12-3: Process Query Suggestions

After the suggestions are imported, they will not appear until they are processed. They are processed via a timer job in SharePoint.

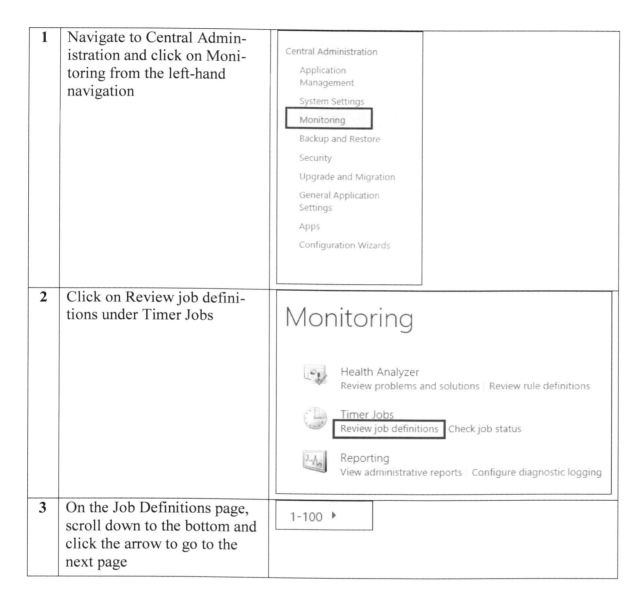

1	Navigate to Central Administration and click on Monitoring from the left-hand navigation	
2	Click on Review job definitions under Timer Jobs	
3	On the Job Definitions page, scroll down to the bottom and click the arrow to go to the next page	

4	Scroll up on the next page and click on the Prepare Query Suggestions	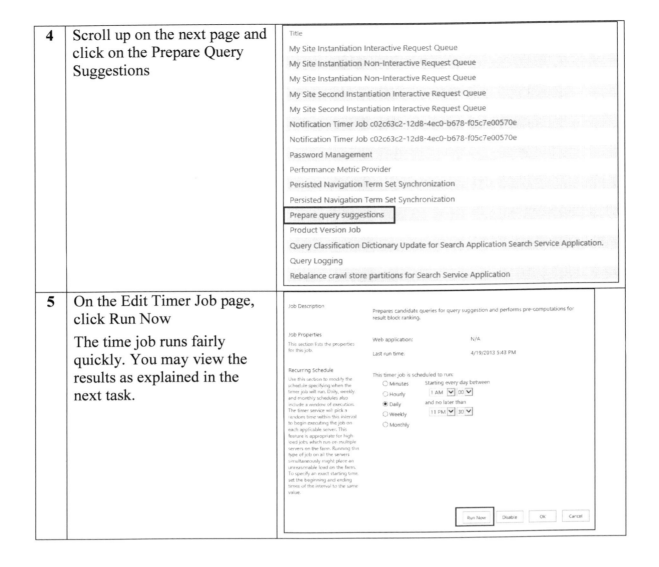
5	On the Edit Timer Job page, click Run Now The time job runs fairly quickly. You may view the results as explained in the next task.	

Task 12-5: View Suggestion Results

1	Navigate to your Search Center and type in a few letters that match some of your suggestion words/phrases	
	The matching suggestions appear under the Search Box. You may modify the suggestion behavior as explained in the next task.	

Task 12-6: Modify Suggestion Behavior

The Search Box web part on each results page in your Search Center may be modified to change the behavior of suggestions.

| 1 | Edit the Search Box web part and expand the Query Suggestions section

For example purposes change the minimum characters to 1 and the suggestions delay to 50 milliseconds. This allows the suggestions to appear quicker. | page.
⊟ Query Suggestions   Help
   ☑ Show suggestions
   ☐ Show people name suggestions

Number of query suggestions
`5`

Minimum number of characters
`1`

Suggestions delay (in milliseconds)
`50`   ✕ | |

Synonyms (Thesaurus)

This lab explains synonyms and shows you how to add your own list of synonyms to SharePoint search.

Synonyms Overview

When people search for items, they may use familiar terms or acronyms accordingly. However, the content may have terms spelled out or contain similar words as the search term but not the same word.

For example, if you search for "Philadelphia" but some content uses "Philly", you won't see those results. Similarly, if you search for "GE" but some content uses "General Electric", you won't see those results either.

This is where synonyms come into play. You may generate and upload a thesaurus file that contains pairs of terms such that when the first term is searched, the second term is also searched.

Task 13-1: Create a Thesaurus File

A thesaurus file is a comma separated file which contains three columns Key, Synonym, and Language. The Language column is optional and therefore your file technically could only contain pairs of synonyms.

An example of thesaurus file contents is as follows

Key,Synonym,Language

IE,Internet Explorer

Internet Explorer,IE

HR, Human Resources

Human Resources, HR

Notice there is no "vice-versa" implied and therefore for each pair you may want to include the opposite order. Think of it as "when I search for this", "also include this".

1	To create a thesaurus file, simply open a text editor, add the header, and then go to town adding pairs of synonyms	synonyms.txt - Notepad File Edit Format View Help Key,Synonym,Language IE,Internet Explorer Internet Explorer,IE HR,Human Resources Human Resources,HR Philadelphia,Philly Philly, Philadelphia Bicycle,Bike Bike,Bicycle
2	Save the file as a .csv file.	

Task 13-2: Import a Thesaurus File

In order to import your thesaurus file, you need to use PowerShell.

1	Launch the SharePoint 2013 Management Console and enter the following two command lines (using your own path for the -FileName parameter) The thesaurus file is imported.	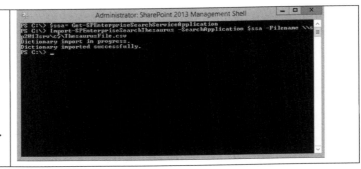

$sssa= Get-SPEnterpriseSearchServiceApplication

Import-SPEnterpriseSearchThesaurus -SearchApplication $ssa -Filename \\sp2013srv\c$\ThesaurusFile.csv

Task 13-3: Test Synonyms in Search

| 1 | To test the thesaurus file, simply search for various synonyms that the file contains.

The example shown uses "bicycle" as a synonym for "bike". | bicycle ⌕

Everything People Conversations Videos Products ···

Relevance ▾

Product Number: SO-B909-L
Product Name: Mountain Bike Socks, L
Product Model: Mountain Bike Socks
Product Category: Clothing

Product Number: BK-R93R-62
Product Name: Road-150 Red, 62
Product Model: Road-150
Product Category: Bikes

Product Number: BK-R93R-44
Product Name: Road-150 Red, 44
Product Model: Road-150
Product Category: Bikes

Product Number: BK-R93R-48
Product Name: Road-150 Red, 48
Product Model: Road-150
Product Category: Bikes

Product Number: BK-R93R-52
Product Name: Road-150 Red, 52
Product Model: Road-150
Product Category: Bikes |

LAB 14

Selective Full Crawls

This lab walks you through several options in performing selective full crawls. Selective full crawls are accomplished by flagging content to be re-indexed. Often times in the past, when you wanted to re-index certain content, you needed to reset all crawled content and then perform a full crawl. Now, you can be more selective and perform re-indexing without having to clear all of the content or perform a full crawl.

Task 14-1: Reindex a Site

1	You may reindex a site (not an entire site collection) by first navigating to the site and selecting Site settings from the Settings menu	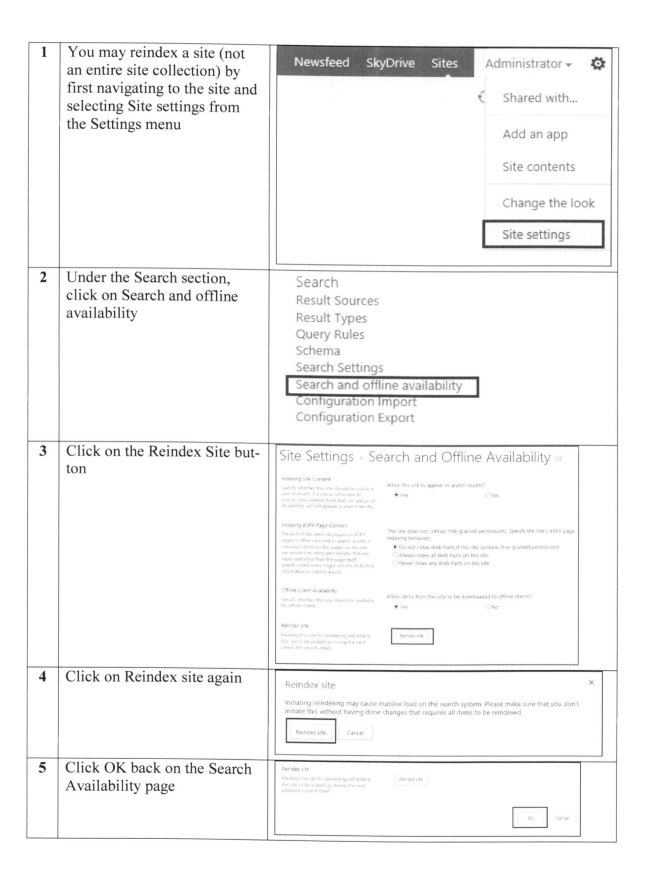
2	Under the Search section, click on Search and offline availability	
3	Click on the Reindex Site button	
4	Click on Reindex site again	
5	Click OK back on the Search Availability page	

| 6 | In your Search Service Application, run an incremental crawl on Local SharePoint Sites

The site is reindexed and crawled fresh. | New Content Source \| Refresh \| ▶ Start all crawls

Type   Name

[icon]   Local SharePoint sites   ▼
[icon]   Products

Edit

View Crawl Log

Start Full Crawl

Start Incremental Crawl

Resume Crawl

Pause Crawl

Stop Crawl

Delete |

Task 14-2: Reindex a Document Library

1	You may reindex a document library by first navigating to the site and selecting Library Settings from the Library top ribbon	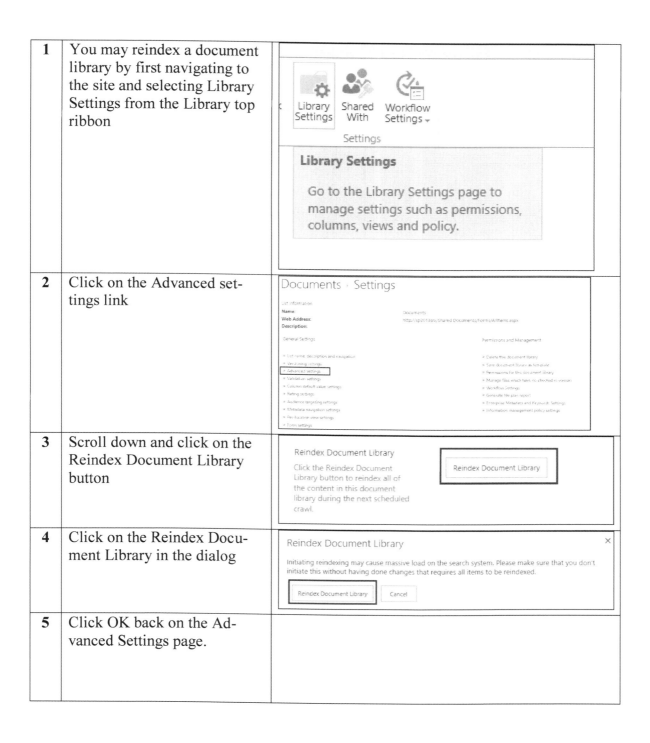
2	Click on the Advanced settings link	
3	Scroll down and click on the Reindex Document Library button	
4	Click on the Reindex Document Library in the dialog	
5	Click OK back on the Advanced Settings page.	

| 6 | In your Search Service Application, run an incremental crawl on Local SharePoint Sites

The document library is reindexed and crawled fresh. | New Content Source \| Refresh \| ▶ Start all crawls

Type   Name

[icon]   Local SharePoint sites   ▾

[icon]   Products   Edit

View Crawl Log

Start Full Crawl

Start Incremental Crawl

Resume Crawl

Pause Crawl

Stop Crawl

Delete |

6028972R00089

Printed in Great Britain
by Amazon.co.uk, Ltd.,
Marston Gate.